1985

Recreation
for the Disabled Child

Recreation
for the
Disabled Child

Donna B. Bernhardt, Editor

The Haworth Press
New York

Recreation for the Disabled Child has also been published as *Physical & Occupational Therapy in Pediatrics,* Volume 4, Number 3, Fall 1984.

The Haworth Press, Inc., 28 East 22 Street, New York, NY 10010

Library of Congress Cataloging in Publication Data
Main entry under title:

Recreation for the disabled child.

    "Has also been published as Physical & occupational therapy in pediatrics, volume 4, number 3, fall 1984"—T.p. verso.
    Includes bibliographies.
    1. Handicapped children—United States—Recreation—Addresses, essays, lectures.
2. Physical education for handicapped children—United States—Addresses, essays, lectures. I.
Bernhardt, Donna B. [DNLM: 1. Handicapped. 2. Recreation. 3. Rehabilitation— in infancy &
childhood. W1 PH683P v.4 no.3 / QT 250 R311d]
GV183.6.R434   615.8'5153   84-19330
ISBN 0-86656-263-X

Recreation
for the Disabled Child

Physical & Occupational Therapy in Pediatrics
Volume 4, Number 3

CONTENTS

Message From the Editor   1
    Donna B. Bernhardt, MS, RPT, ATC

Rehabilitation: Expanding the Definition   3
    Lyle J. Micheli, MD

The Therapeutics of Recreation   9
    Margaret M. Klein, RPT

Exercise Testing and Training for Disabled Populations:
The State of the Art   13
    Donna B. Bernhardt, MS, RPT, ATC

  Spinal Cord Injury   13
  Amputation   16
  Cerebral Palsy   17
  Chronic Pulmonary Diseases   18
  Cardiac Disease   20
  Diabetes   22
  Blindness   22
  Conclusion   23

Handicapped Skiing: A Current Review of Downhill Snow
Skiing for the Disabled   27
    David P. McCormick, MD

  The Handicapped Ski Club   27
  Students   30
  Adaptive Equipment   30
  Ski School   32
  Amputee Skiing   35
  Blind Skiing   38
  Safety Considerations   42
  Fitness   42

Running for Therapy   45
    Elizabeth Stevenson, EdD, RPT, ACT, CCT

  Physiological Effects of Running   46
  Summary   53
  Conditioning for Running   53
  Running and the Disabled   56
  Alternatives to Running   60
  Summary   61

Team Sports   65
    Barney F. LeVeau, PhD, LPT

  Needs or Motivational Drives   65
  Anxieties or Fears   67
  Role of Leaders   68
  General Objectives   70
  Modification of Team Sports   73
  Summary   75

The Competitive Spirit   77
    Donna B. Bernhardt, MS, RPT, ATC

  National Events   77
  International Events   81
  Conclusions   83

Body Image and Physical Activity   85
    John M. Silva III, PhD
    Jennifer Klatsky

  Body Image as a Psychosocial Phenomenon   86
  Malleability of the Body Image   87
  Structuring a Program   89

BOOK REVIEWS

Sports Medicine—Fitness, Training, Injuries, ed 2, edited by O.
Appenzeller and R. Atkinson   93
    Reviewed by Donna B. Bernhardt, MS, RPT,
    ATC

Adapted Physical Education: A Practitioner's Guide, by L.F.
Masters, A.A. Mori, and E.K. Lange   94
    Reviewed by Donna B. Bernhardt, MS, RPT,
    ATC

Recreation Experiences for the Severely Impaired or Non-Ambulatory Child, by S.P. Levine, N. Sharow, C. Gaudette, and S. Spector   96
          Reviewed by Elizabeth Stevenson, EdD, RPT, ATC, CCT

Sports for the Handicapped, by A. Allen   97
          Reviewed by David J. Miller, MS, LPT

Symposium on Pediatric and Adolescent Sports Medicine, edited by J.M. Betts and M. Eichelberger   97
          Reviewed by Michael T. Gross, MS, LPT

Don't Feel Sorry for Paul, by B. Wolfe   98
          Reviewed by Ruth Walker, LPT

Recreational Resources   **101**
          Donna B. Bernhardt, MS, RPT, ATC

Equipment   101
Programs   103
Audiovisuals—Publications   107

MARLYS M. MITCHELL, PhD, OTR, *Professor, Division of Occupational Therapy, Department of Medical Allied Health Professions, University of North Carolina at Chapel Hill*

PATRICIA C. MONTGOMERY, PhD, RPT, *Pediatric Physical Therapy Services, St. Louis Park, MN*

MARTHA C. PIPER, PhD, *Associate Professor and Director, School of Physical and Occupational Therapy, McGill University, Montreal, Quebec, Canada*

HEINZ F.R. PRECHTL, *Professor and Chairman, Department of Developmental Neurology, University Hospital, Groningen, The Netherlands*

DONALD K. ROUTH, PhD, *Professor, Department of Psychology, The University of Iowa*

MARILYN SEIF, MS, *Speech Pathologist, Marshfield Clinic, Marshfield, WI*

GEORGIA M. SHAMBES, PhD, *Professor, Program in Physical Therapy, School of Allied Health Professions, University of Wisconsin-Madison*

EARL SIEGEL, MD, *Professor of Maternal and Child Health; Clinical Professor of Pediatrics University of North Carolina at Chapel Hill*

NAPOLEON WOLANSKI, PhD, DSc, *Head Department of Human Ecology of the Polish Academy of Sciences, Warsaw, Poland*

JANET E. YOUNG, MD, RPT, *Chief, Development Pediatric Section, Department of Pediatrics, Fitzsimmons Army Medical Center, Aurora, CO*

MESSAGE FROM THE EDITOR

Mainstreaming has been broadly defined as the integration or reintegration of special populations into a lifestyle that is active and productive, both personally and professionally. The ultimate intent is to make all people a cohesive circle regardless of their physical or mental dissimilarities.

For many years I believed that I was mainstreaming the children, adolescents and young adults with whom I worked. I was using therapeutic intervention to place my charges back in family structures, in school situations or in work environments. The questions and pursuits of my patients taught me differently. These individuals were not content just to go home and attend school or work. They also desired to participate in recreation. Thus began my quest to discover the athletic capacities and skills of a variety of disability groups.

At the initiation of this search, questions were far more numerous than answers. Little research or athletic programming had addressed the area of recreation for special individuals. Enthusiasm and improvisation were our strongest tools. Gradually, a network of people, both able-bodied and disabled, who had interest or expertise in many areas of athletic pursuit, began to emerge.

This special issue is the culmination of the care, interest and enthusiasm of many of those persons who desire to mainstream totally our special populations. The research and programs included represent only the tip of the iceberg. Much more scientific study, education and community involvement are necessary for mainstreaming in recreation to be successful.

I hope that you, the readers, will use this information as a springboard for further solutions. A disability will not become a handicap if solutions to the problems occasioned by the disability can be found.

Donna B. Bernhardt, MS, RPT, ATC
Guest Editor

Rehabilitation:
Expanding the Definition

Lyle J. Micheli, MD

Rehabilitative medicine as a formal discipline is a relatively new addition to traditional medical specialities. Heroic individual efforts have been made to improve the functional potential of the handicapped. These efforts began primarily in the 19th century in Europe with notable pioneers such as Louis Braille, Maria Montessori, and Jean Jacques Rousseau.[1] The particular contribution of American medicine, however, has been to systemize the case of the handicapped and to include a great variety of specialists, such as engineers, speech therapists, audiologists, psychiatrists, psychologists, and dance therapists in the total management of the handicapped child or adult. Thus, what characterizes the most recent approaches to the care of the disabled is the increased level of organization and the more inclusive plan of care. The end result has been a team concept with individuals from various disciplines coordinating their efforts to assist the handicapped.

In the United States, the impetus to systematically assess the disabilities of an individual and to design approaches to improve his functional level through special learning programs, assistive devices, or exercise programs, has come primarily from two very different disciplines, pediatric medicine and military medicine. The care of children with physical disabilities resulting from hereditary or drug induced defects, cerebral palsy, or certain of the childhood acquired diseases such as poliomyelitis, received early attention. The first major organized approach to studying (handicapped children) and meeting the needs was spearheaded by Franklin Delano Roosevelt. A polio victim himself, he founded the National Foundation for Infantile Paralysis in the mid-1930's. A direct result of this national attention was the formation of the Crippled Children's Services in most states. These services were specifically structured to provide orthopaedic and medical care to handicapped children. The early Crippled Children's Services devoted much of their attention to three ma-

Dr. Micheli is Instructor in Orthopaedic Surgery, Harvard Medical School and Associate in the Department of Orthopaedic Surgery, The Children's Hospital, Boston, Massachusetts.

3

jor areas—corrective surgery, primarily of musculoskeletal disorders, bracing and splinting, and physical therapy to maintain strength and function of the extremities. These efforts continue to this day. The immediate goals in the management of these children with musculoskeletal or neuro-muscular disorders were, admittedly, of a limited nature. The basic objective was to help the child attain the functional level of "community ambulator." This level entailed the ability of the individual to move about the community under her own locomotion and perform independent functions of daily living including, if possible, household and work activities.

A much more comprehensive approach to the handicapped resulted from two recent pieces of federal legislation. The first, incorporated in Section 504 of the Rehabilitation Act of 1973, provided that no discrimination be permitted against any group, including the handicapped, in federally financed programs. The act legislated access for all people to physical space or educational facilities. The second, much more specifically directed to the handicapped, was Public Law 94-142, the Education for All Handicapped Children Act, passed in 1975. As a result of this law and its interpretations, a handicapped child had the right to be assessed by an "individualized education program committee" (IEC) in order to implement the "free appropriate education guarantee" (FAPE) which was secured by the law. The implementation of this wide-reaching law ultimately popularized the development of a specific committee consisting of physical therapists, occupational therapists, speech pathologists, nurses, social workers and psychologists, as well as physicians, to provide a multifaceted approach to meet the needs of the handicapped child. As a result of Public Law 94-142, not only are the musculoskeletal problems of the handicapped addressed. The physical and cognitive problems of multi-handicapped children and their complete educational needs, including their physical education and sports needs are additionally evaluated.[2]

Hence, the most recent and necessary addition to the care team for the handicapped child has been the physical educator or sports coach with specific skills and interests in sports and fitness programs for the handicapped. These programs go one step beyond pure physical therapy. While many of the games or dance movements may incorporate therapeutic exercises in their patterns, the structure is indeed that of game or sport and, as such, requires the special skills of the sports specialist.

The care of the handicapped with acquired injuries from military activity has also undergone progressive development and sophistication. Military activities in both World Wars I and II, as well as the Korean and Vietnamese campaigns, created large numbers of acquired handicaps of vision, hearing and ambulation. The majority of ambulation deficits resulted from amputation or neurological impairment.

Dramatic developments were made in both the military hospitals and the Veterans Administration in prosthetic and orthotic design, as well as in the development of rehabilitative services and programs for the spinal cord injured and the amputee. While the initial primary goal of rehabilitation was, once again, to attain the level of "community ambulator," many people soon recognized that handicapped servicemen had many other emotional and social needs which required additional attention if they were to return to community life as active participants.[3]

As comprehensive as many of these military rehabilitation programs were, they often fell short of providing opportunities for function beyond the "community ambulator" stage. As a former patient noted, the object seemed to be to enable one to walk sufficiently well to get to the bathroom and kitchen. Any additional function beyond that level was considered a bonus and beyond the concern of the rehabilitation facility.

In particular, sports activity, if considered at all, was seen primarily as a diversionary function. Too often, the broken prosthesis or damaged wheelchair was reason enough to barely tolerate or actively discourage sports activity by the child or young adult with a disability.

Definite exceptions to this approach, however, did occur. Kerr and Brunnstrom, in their 1956 text on training of the lower extremity amputee, reported on a study at several military hospitals in which amputees were rehabilitated using dancing training. This study concluded that the amputees attained functional levels from these dancing programs at a more rapid rate than from regular training programs.[4]

The era of the Vietnam conflict, with an unusually high number of lower extremity injuries in our military personnel, ushered in a more comprehensive approach to military rehabilitation, including the return to or participation in sports activities as one of the criteria for rehabilitation. The Veterans Administration Hospital in Boulder, Colorado was instrumental in the early development of handicapped skiing and riding programs for the amputee. This program, in turn, was actively expanded to the civilian population including pediatric groups with acquired amputations.[5]

A number of additional contributions have strengthened this altered concept of rehabilitation which includes active sports participation as a component of the rehabilitative process. Technical advances in the design of wheelchairs, prosthetics, outrigger skis, and special weight training machines have made sports a mechanical possibility. Additionally, the development of special rules and techniques in both sport and dance have resulted from the participation of interested coaches and dance teachers.

Therapeutic exercises aimed at improving the range of motion, developing strength or coordination of a child in the more traditional milieu of the hospital or out-patient physical therapy unit, have sometimes been perceived as laborious, potentially painful, or "boring." The same exercises, when incorporated into a competitive sports or dance program, or "work-out" session in a fitness center, may become a challenge to be

mastered or a source of active enjoyment to be pursued by the participants. In a recent conference on dance medicine held in North Carolina,
programs as diverse as dance exercise for children with cerebral palsy
and dance therapy for geriatric amputees were described.[6] The enthusiasm of the participants was matched only by the enthusiasm of the
teachers and coaches.

Much of the impetus for this new development of specific sports programs for the handicapped has come from the handicapped themselves.
The development of special ski equipment, light weight pylons for canoeing or kayaking, and light weight low friction wheelchairs made from
thermoplastics and aluminum, are a few examples of equipment designed
from client demand.

While the primary responsibility for the continued development of
competitive sports programs for the handicapped should remain the responsibility of the handicapped sportsmen themselves, the medical and
sports communities must also share the responsibility to ensure the safe
and physiologically sound development of these sports programs. The
physician, sports scientist, or physical educator who assesses the physical
and psychological status of a given individual, including his "fitness
level," must always consider any other special anatomic or physiologic
limitations which the individual may have before preparing the "exercise
prescription" and before recommending any exercises, sport, or physical
activity. An example of the special care which must be taken in developing such sports programs can be seen in the Special Olympic movement.
Medical literature has documented that children with Down's syndrome
may have an increased laxity at the upper cervical spine which may place
them at special risk of injury in sports participation.[7] The sports medical
personnel involved in such programs have the responsibility to screen
properly the participants and to ensure that children who are at special
risk of such instability, as demonstrated by careful medical assessment,
are protected from injury. The purpose of such careful sports medical
supervision, of course, is to ensure the safety of the participants while
avoiding unnecessary limitations upon participation. The object should be
to recommend a rate and intensity of training which will improve performance and health, while avoiding injury.

Hence, the preparation of the exercise prescription for handicapped individuals is really no different from the process with able-bodied persons.
It may simply require additional expertise for its formulation. The input
of the bioengineer, sports psychologist, or certain medical specialists
such as neurologists or cardiologists, may be required to supervise at
competitions and to make recommendations for intensity of the training.

Despite these recent advances in the development of programs and
competitions for the disabled, more research to determine ways to maximize the benefits of sports and exercise programs for the disabled must be

done. Two examples readily come to mind. Multiple sclerosis is a neurologic disorder of unknown etiology which results in loss of coordination, muscle strength, flexibility and locomotor function. Traditionally, simple therapeutic exercises and the avoidance of over-fatigue have been the primary recommendations given to individuals with this condition, however, a number of individuals with multiple sclerosis were quite dissatisfied with the very cautious approach of the medical establishment. They reported in their own cases an apparent improvement in physical function and in the sense of self-fulfillment, from participation in vigorous sports or fitness training exercise programs. Former olympic skier Jimmy Huega, in particular, called the attention of the National Multiple Sclerosis Foundation to the need for clearer guidelines for sports and exercise for individuals with this condition. As a result of this concern, a team of individuals prepared a manual which gives guidelines for sports and exercise participation for the individual with multiple sclerosis.[8] These guidelines include systematic and symmetric synchronous exercises such as biking or swimming as well as simple techniques for avoiding injury while exercising.

While much research remains to be done to determine the actual benefit or lack of benefit of regular exercise of the neuromuscular system in this condition, the publication of this "exercise book" represents an important first step in recognition of the importance of fitness and exerc se in such conditions. Much of this exercise prescription for multiple sclerosis is at present based solely on clinical impressions: a heated environment seems to increase fatigue and possibly overheating; most structured exercise techniques should be done in a supportive environment on a stationary bike or treadmill with handgrips because of the frequent involvement of the cerebellum in this condition; the need exists for very slow progression of exercise intensity since the patient has been deconditioned by the disease process. Hopefully, this "empiric" approach to the use of exercise in this condition will serve as a further impetus to the study of human performance and enhancement of this performance in the face of this disease process.

Another handicapping disease process in which many questions remain about the formulation of the exercise prescription is muscular dystrophy. Although, once again, therapeutic exercise has had a place in the care of a child with muscular dystrophy, a strong emphasis has never been placed on progressive resistive exercises. Instead, the therapeutic exercises have generally been of the low resistance type with primary emphasis on the prevention of joint contractures and the maintenance of endurance type motion.

While the use in dystrophic disease of progressive resistive exercises incorporating an "over-load" of the remaining healthy motor units of primary muscle seems logical, and was the basis of much of the work in the rehabilitation of patients afflicted with poliomyelitis, it has never received strong impetus in the management of children or young adults. Yet, several patients with muscular dystrophy have made rather dramatic improvements in their function with the use of resistive weight training utilizing free weights, Nautilus equipment, or isotonic techniques. These rehabilitative techniques have been used primarily in rehabilitation of injured athletes or active individuals, but the potential for their use in individuals with muscle disease would appear to be very worthy of careful study.

In summary, much research remains to be done in the study of sports and exercise activity for the handicapped. Initial clinical observations have, in general, given strong impetus to the further exploration of ways in which sports and exercise could be incorporated into the rehabilitation and ongoing support systems for the child or adult with a handicapping condition. Coaches, physical educators, and sports medicine specialists are now part of the handicapped care team, and continue to encourage the definition and utilization of sports as a portion of the rehabilitation process.

REFERENCES

1. Switzer M E : Rehabilitation social legislation. in *Industrial Society Rehabilitation—Problems and Solutions.* ISRD - Proceedings of the 10th World Congress, Weisbaden, Germany, September 11-17, 1966.

2. Fraser B A, Hensinger R N : The seriously handicapped population: Society's response to their needs and problems, in *Managing Physical Handicaps: A Practical Guide for Parents, Care Providers and Educators.* (Baltimore:) Paul H Brookes Publishing Company, 1983.

3. Dawson A R, Knudson A B C : The importance of physical medicine and rehabilitation as demonstrated by the experience of the Veterans Administration, in Soden, WH (ed): *Rehabilitation of the Handicapped.* (New York:) Ronald Press Company, 1949.

4. Kerr D, Brunnstrom S : Social dancing and sports, in *Training of the Lower Extremity Amputee.* (Springfield, IL:) Charles C Thomas Publisher, 1956.

5. *Adjusted Sports in the Veterans Administration.* (Washington, DC,) Special Service Information Bulletin IB 6-252 Recreation Service, Veterans Administration.

6. (Neuromuscular Performance), North Carolina Physical Therapy Association Conference, (Winston-Salem, NC:) June 4-6, 1982.

7. Semine A A, Ertel A N, Goldberg M J, et al.: Cervical spine instability in children with Downs Syndrome. *J Bone Jt Surg* 60A:649, 1978.

8. Frankel D, Baxbaum R (eds): *Maximizing Your Health.* (Waltham, MA:) National Multiple Sclerosis Society Massachusetts Chapter, 1982.

The Therapeutics of Recreation

Margaret M. Klein, RPT

Increase range of motion, decrease pain, promote independence in activities of daily living, improve gait pattern, prevent contractures, improve functional status, correct posture and body mechanics, encourage relaxation, increase muscle strength and flexibility, increase endurance, improve balance and coordination, inhibit reflex patterns, decrease spasticity, stimulate developmental growth sequence, increase muscle tone, general conditioning, prevention of injury . . .

These are the short and long term goals of physical and occupational therapy; the specific goals for our patients, who are all "physically disabled," whether temporarily or chronically. In actuality, these are all short term goals in preparation for the long term goal we attempt to achieve—the enhancement of life. This enhancement is our ultimate therapeutic goal.

What are the means to achieve this goal? Increase range, decrease pain, functional independence in daily activities. Elements of all the methods are required, but more is necessary.

Consider the treatment frequency and duration indicated to achieve our long term goal. When do we begin to enhance life? Is it only to be pursued twice per week for two to four weeks or three times per week for two weeks? As physical and occupational therapists we have the tools from our professional education and experience to assist our patients in attaining this constant, lifetime goal. The tool we can use for rehabilitation and education is sport and recreation. With extensive background and training in anatomy and kinesiology, neurology, physiology, developmental growth, gerontology, medical science and pathology, therapists have exactly what is required.

Exercise and sport have much greater value than mere leisure activity. When combined with therapeutic needs, they can become an enjoyable

---

Ms. Klein is an independent consultant in recreation with disabled persons and Home Care Physical Therapist, Fairview Hospital, Minneapolis, MN.

and exciting means to that long term goal. Instead of a wand or dowel, imagine lifting a canoe paddle for shoulder range of motion. The weight can be adjusted by using a lighter paddle or strapping a weight to the shaft of the paddle. As the person begins to learn different strokes, we observe eye-hand coordination, right-left coordination and integration, the crossing of midline, weight-shift, and sitting balance. Once in the water, upper extremity strengthening begins. The size of the paddle and depth of the stroke determine the degree of difficulty. As the boat begins to move, communication, socialization, *functional* purpose and progress are added to our list of therapeutic benefits.

For many people with chronic physical disability, life is often sheltered and risk-free. Physical activity can offer them an opportunity for excitement and challenge. Consider the teenaged skier with a spinal-cord injury practicing transfers from a wheelchair to a pulk sled. As winter snows approach, training (i.e., therapy) includes upper body strengthening, flexibility and endurance exercises; lower extremity skin care and range of motion exercises. All these skills prepare the young athlete for pulk skiing which in the United States can be enjoyed for recreational or competitive purposes. Therapeutic short term goals and the ultimate long term goal have been successfully met and enjoyed.

Another example integrates therapeutic needs with sport and recreation for a child with spastic diplegia. Among the short term therapeutic goals are reduction in hip adductor spasticity and improvement in balance and coordination. Consider horseback riding. Once mounted, the gentle rocking rhythm of the horse in combination with his body warmth contacting the child's adductor muscles bring about a gentle relaxation of those spastic muscles. Think also of the balance and coordination required just to sit on a horse. The upright posture, the two-handed coordination, the weight-shift; therapeutic benefits are multiple and varied. For many disabled people horseback riding can also serve as a vehicle into remote wilderness and mountain regions that are otherwise inaccessible. A view of life different than from a wheelchair provides an enhancing life experience . . . and therapy continues all the while.

For coaches and instructors who may not understand the medical background or therapeutic needs of their players, the therapist can be a welcome educator. Besides calming the apprehensions of an individual making initial contact with a physically disabled person, the therapist may advise in positioning, lifting and handling techniques as well as technical skills and training methods. For example, a youth who enjoyed weight training suffers a closed head injury with resulting spasticity. He wants longingly to return to the weight room yet is forewarned not to mistakenly strengthen spastic muscles. With the guidance of a physical therapist various neurodevelopmental positions for inhibiting spasticity are applied and the young man soon joins his friends in an activity he loves. Social and recreational needs are met as well as the functional therapeutic need of inhibiting spasticity.

When the patient is medically stable, we can begin implementing the long term goal, life enhancement. While doing the initial assessment, concentrate on the patient's *functional* abilities. What activities has the patient done? What is he or she doing now and what would he or she wish to learn? What are the therapeutic needs of the individual? The activity should be chosen in relation to specific therapeutic goals. What must the patient have or be able to learn in order to participate? Finally, proceed with pertinent testing for the necessary information to place the patient into the activity. The functional tests may include gross or specific manual muscle testing, range of motion, sitting-standing balance, coordination, gait and mobility assessment, endurance, posture, leg length, grip strength and many more. In addition, take note of any adaptive equipment the patient may presently use or need for the desired activity.

We cannot assume that all disabled people are interested in physical exercise; therefore, the individual should be respected and offered the choice to participate in an activity. Not all able-bodied people enjoy sport and recreation; the disabled are no different. Money, transportation and accessibility are all factors requiring consideration; however, the greatest barrier to active participation is the attitude of able-bodied and disabled alike. The therapist plays a most crucial role at this point. We know the capabilities and potential of our patients and have earned their trust and confidence. Most often we are the ones who can suggest and persuade them to pursue a suitable sport, encourage assertiveness and tap their creativity by helping them to find ways to adapt the sport. We may need to be "proddingly" encouraging, developing the attitude that "one never knows until one tries."

We serve an homogenous population in a sense. All our patients are "physically" disabled in some way. Thus, this theory of rehabilitation and education through sport and recreation could apply to all patients we see. The medical profession is not always aware (or convinced) of the benefits of physical recreation and sport. Physical and occupational therapists can serve as a powerful influence in identification and education. We must tap our own knowledge, patience and creativity to assist our patients to reach their long term goal. Hence, we may also come closer to attaining our own long term goal—enhancement of life.

REFERENCES

Dendy, E: Recreation for disabled people—What do we mean? *Physiother* 64: 290-293, 1978
Dendy, E: Recreation for the Disabled—How to go about it. *Physiother* 64: 328-329, 1978

Exercise Testing and Training for Disabled Populations: The State of the Art

Donna B. Bernhardt, MS, RPT, ATC

Physical fitness has become increasingly important to many individuals. One mode frequently selected to improve cardiovascular endurance, muscle strength, and flexibility is involvement in sports.[1] Both able-bodied and disabled people have developed an interest in recreation and sport for health promotion and physical fitness. An explosion of individual and team events for both groups has accompanied this heightened interest.

This surge of concern for fitness has resulted in the development of research tools to assess physical capacities and exercise limits. The methods most frequently employed to evaluate physiological capacity, the treadmill and the bicycle ergometer, focus on the activation of large muscle mass.[1-5] Using these tools, a considerable amount of data has been compiled on the exercise capacity of able-bodied persons. Persons with a physical disability are frequently unable to perform standardized tests; thus, scant data exist on the response to and the capacity for exercise in most disabled groups.

The purpose of this paper is to present the viable testing alternatives that have been used with various disability groups and to summarize the current findings relative to the exercise capacity of these groups.

SPINAL CORD INJURY

Investigators have developed several types of ergometers, or instruments which measure active work done on a stationary piece of equipment, for upper body stress testing. These devices are the forearm (arm-crank) ergometer, the wheelchair ergometer, and freewheeling on a treadmill.

Donna B. Bernhardt is Assistant Professor, Boston University, Sargent College of Allied Health Professions, University Road, Boston, MA 02215.

The forearm ergometer is a non-specific stressor of the cardiopulmonary system. Portability and low cost often offset the lack of task specificity to wheelchair propulsion.[6] Bar-Or and Zwiren[7] tested fifty-nine males on treadmill and arm crank ergometry to assess the reliability and validity of arm testing. Maximal oxygen uptake ($\dot{V}O_2$ max) and minute ventilation (V_e) demonstrated reliability of .94 and .98 respectively during arm cranking, while maximal heart rate (HR max) was less consistent (r = .76). The arm test was a valid predictor of maximal capacity with values consistently 65% of the treadmill values.

The exercise capacity of the spinal-cord injured (SCI) has been traditionally assessed on forearm ergometry. Hulleman et al.[8] used arm cranking and telemetry to determine cardiovascular and pulmonary efficiency in various sports and disability levels. Vital capacity, $\dot{V}O_2$ max, and physical work capacity (PWC) increased as disability decreased. Maximal blood pressure (BP) averaged 165/93 mmHG and HR max was 153 in all classes. The highest pulse frequency was noted in the dash, slalom and swim competitions, while weight lifters exhibited the greatest tachycardia.

In their classic study Zwiren and Bar-Or[9] evaluated paraplegic and normal males who differed in conditioning level on a continuous progressive arm test. $\dot{V}O_2$ and VE at maximal level were similar for normal and wheelchair athletes, but higher than comparable results from normal and wheelchair sedentary males. Submaximal heart rate was lower in athletes, while submaximal oxygen consumption demonstrated a similar pattern to maximal levels. The authors concluded that activity level rather than disability determines exercise response.

Wolf and Magore[10] examined the results of physical effort and postural changes on responses of different levels of spinal lesions. They reported normal electrocardiograph responses in all patients. Responses of blood pressure and heart rate were normal in low level paraplegics. Blood pressure dropped in the erect posture and in exercise in high level paraplegics and quadriplegics. Heart rate increased with upright posture and exercise in high level paraplegics, but showed only slight changes with exercise in quadriplegics. Hjeltnes[11] demonstrated normal $\dot{V}O_2$ max and pulmonary function in discontinuous exercise in low level paraplegics. Cardiac output was lower in a majority of the paraplegics, possibly secondary to hypokinetic circulation from loss of vasomotor regulation. A lower stroke volume, higher heart rate and blood lactate further suggested a sluggish regional circulation. He concluded that spinal lesion does not affect upper extremity efficiency, but does alter cardiovascular dynamics. Nilsson, Staff and Pruett[12] likewise recorded similar exercise responses for adult paraplegic and normal males with the exception of a greater HR max in the paraplegics.

In an effort to address the issue of task specificity in testing, many researchers have devised variations of wheelchair propulsion for laboratory data collection. Early wheelchair ergometers consisted of a special platform with pairs of low friction rollers on which the wheelchair rested. Later versions have mounted wheelchairs on a treadmill or have linked through a stationary wheelchair to a bicycle or other external flywheel. Glaser et al.[13] and Stoboy, Rich and Lee[14] have validated the exercise specificity and clinical suitability of the wheelchair ergometer.

Assessment of physiological capacity on wheelchair ergometers has been researched by several investigators. Voight and Bahn[15] demonstrated similar relationships in metabolic rate, $\dot{V}O_2$ max, and heart rate during wheelchair treadmill work of able-bodied and paralysed individuals. Brauer[16] and Knowlton, Fitzgerald and Sedlock[17] evaluated able-bodied and wheelchair dependent persons on wheelchair ergometers. Both studies demonstrated parallel increases in heart rate, energy expenditure, and push rates as workload increased in both groups. $\dot{V}O_2$ max and maximal power output were also closely matched. The one interesting finding in both studies was that the wheelchair persons demonstrated greater mechanical efficiency at increasing workloads, possibly because of a training effect or familiarity with the activity.

Comparisons of arm cranking and wheelchair ergometry have been made to evaluate which method is more effective for testing individuals in wheelchairs. Wicks et al.[18] demonstrated no significant differences in $\dot{V}O_2$, heart rate and ventilation volume at maximal exercise levels. Glaser et al.[19] repeated Wick's study with more equivalent workloads. They demonstrated greater work capacity, heart rates and blood lactate for arm cranking, but correlations were fairly high (work r = 0.86, heart rate r = 0.72, blood lactate r = 0.52, $\dot{V}O_2$ max r = 0.92). Glaser et al.[20] demonstrated greater metabolic and cardiopulmonary responses in wheelchair ergometry at submaximal levels, suggesting that the inefficient biomechanics and smaller upper body musculature are involved in wheelchair propulsion. Brattgard, Grimby and Hook[21] assessed able-bodied women on the arm crank and wheelchair ergometers. They demonstrated the arm crank to be twice as efficient at several workloads. Glaser et al.[22] further indicated that synchronous wheeling is less efficient than asynchronous wheeling. These differences in efficiency have been attributed to utilization of different muscle groups for work and stabilization, neural predisposition to asychrony or mechanical differences in gears and cranks.[6]

Available data indicate that training the cardiorespiratory system of wheelchair-dependent individuals is quite possible. Engle and Hildebrandt[23] demonstrated a significant training effect in thirteen paraplegics following fourteen weeks of vigorous physical therapy and wheelchair ergometry. Heart rates decreased an average of 20 beats per minute at rest and in absolute work. Dreisinger[24] elicited increases in power output and $\dot{V}O_2$ max after twenty weeks of forearm training, while DiCarlo, Supp and Taylor[26] described a 60% increase in $\dot{V}O_2$ after five weeks of training.

Increases in $\dot{V}O_2$ max, minute ventilation and wheelchair treadmill time were noted by Gass et al.[27] in seven high level paraplegics after seven weeks of training. A 12% increase in $\dot{V}O_2$ max, a 31% increases in performance as well as improvements in efficiency and strength were recorded by Nilsson, Staff and Pruett[12] following a similar seven week training period.

In conclusion, the research data indicate that wheelchair individuals respond to increasing workloads with linear increases in oxygen uptake, minute ventilation and heart rate. Efficiency also increases with power output to a point of muscular fatigue. Training appears to affect the cardiorespiratory variables at both submaximal and maximal levels.

AMPUTATION

Scant research has addressed the physiological capacity of persons with amputations. Most investigators have used laboratory equipment to assess either the metabolic cost of walking with prosthesis versus crutches, or to evaluate the energy cost of ambulation versus wheelchair propulsion. Molen[28] studied the relationship of energy to speed in fifty-four below-knee amputees. He documented 20% increases in $\dot{V}O_2$ of the amputees when compared to predictions. Speed correlated positively with energy cost. Paglierulo, Waters and Hislop,[29] studying the energy cost of prosthetic versus crutch walking, noted greater oxygen uptake and heart rate with crutches. They suggested that prosthetic gait is more efficient, although still 36% more costly than normal ambulation. Free cadence ambulation was shown to be most efficient. Traugh, Corcoran and Reyes[30] studied nine above-knee amputees with various prosthetic conditions and with crutches. Prosthetic cost equalled crutch walking for fair ambulators, but was less for good ambulators. Energy cost was also slightly greater with the knee unlocked versus locked. Use of a wheelchair was less costly than a prosthesis. Huang et al.[31] demonstrated that the energy cost increased as the level of amputation rose.

Few authors have evaluated physical work capacity of amputees on ergometric instruments. In a classic study, James[32] assessed thirty-seven male above-knee amputees during prosthetic walking on a treadmill. Both $\dot{V}O_2$, HR max and blood lactate were greater for the amputees than for able-bodied reference males, indicating a greater metabolic cost of prosthetic gait. A strong linear correlation of oxygen cost and walking weight suggested that the higher energy cost is secondary to greater physical work. James and Nordgren[33] then compared the same subjects on treadmill and single leg bicycle ergometry. Oxygen uptake was 9-12% lower on cycling, but heart rate and blood lactate were greater. The authors concluded that one leg cycling utilized muscle that was untrained for the activity, hence oxygen utilization was less efficient and local ischemia occurred. Comparison of all values to able-bodied predictors showed a lower physical work capacity of the amputees on both tests. The authors stated that the movement handicap results in a lower state of cardiovascular training. Bernhardt[34] compared four males with above-knee amputations to able-bodied males on arm crank and single limb ergometry. $\dot{V}O_2$ max and HR max were similar for both groups on the tests. Net efficiency was lower while mean blood pressure was higher for the amputees on both tests. The author concluded that maximal physiological capacity was unchanged by amputation, but a slower lifestyle reduced efficiency.

Training studies in amputee populations are rare. The one study by James[35] of eleven above-knee amputees following twelve weeks of bicycle and walking training demonstrated 6-7% increases in $\dot{V}O_2$ max, 23% increases in physical work performed and improvement in mechanical efficiency.

In summary, the metabolic cost of amputee ambulation is greater than normal gait. Amputees appear to have similar physiological capacity, but lower efficiency than their able-bodied references. Training does seem to cause positive alterations in cardiovascular variables.

CEREBRAL PALSY

The majority of the research on physiological capacity in persons with motor control difficulties has centered around comparisons to able-bodied persons or comparisons among types of control problems. Lundberg[36] studied nine children and five young adults with spastic cerebral palsy on a bicycle ergometer. Comparison of results to normal controls revealed a 50% reduction in physical work capacity in the disabled group. The author concluded that the extra energy required for stabilization and qualitative changes in muscle reduce efficiency and increase work. Lundberg[37] repeated his research with spastic versus dyskinetic/ataxic subjects to determine if the bicycle ergometer could distinguish any differences in groups. The results demonstrated no significant changes in mechanical efficiency between the dyskinetic and normal controls. The dyskinetic versus spastic groups exhibited great differences, probably secondary to greater energy expenditure by the spastic patients in overcoming muscle tone increases during cycling. Thoren[38] suggested that paretic musculature demonstrated qualitative changes in metabolism and substrate utilization, including mitochondrial changes, decreased blood flow, increased number and activity of Type II fibers, and decreased uptake of oxygen, glucose and free fatty acids.

Several authors have evaluated training effects in children with cerebral palsy. Berg[39] used innovative ergometric instrumentation to assess physical capacity of forty-one adolescents with cerebral palsy. Either sitting or supine bicycle ergometry, tricycle ergometry, or prone saucer ergometry was employed to assess training effects of triweekly exercise sessions. Increases in $\dot{V}O_2$, blood volume and total hemoglobin were noted. The author concluded that improved muscular efficiency accounted for the changes in oxygen consumption. Lundberg and Pernow[40] studied nine males with cerebral palsy before and after a six week training period using large muscle groups. They did not record any changes in $\dot{V}O_2$ max, mechanical efficiency or ventilatory variables; however, increases were noted in physical work capacity and oxygen utilization. A two year program of biweekly training was conducted by Bar-Or et al.[41] with twenty-six cerebral palsy and twenty-one post-polio patients. Testing on an arm ergometer demonstrated slight decreases in submaximal heart rate and improvement in $\dot{V}O_2$ for the cerebral palsy patients. The authors concluded that the program was not strenuous enough for the polio patients.

Thus, research indicates that physiological responses to exercise and training are inconclusive and somewhat contradictory in cerebral palsy groups. Further study is needed to clarify this area.

CHRONIC PULMONARY DISEASES

The exercise capacity of children with bronchial asthma, the most frequent chronic disease of childhood, has been poorly assessed. Physical exertion often induces asthma-like attacks, so testing becomes a difficult problem. Oseid[42] reviewed the pattern and mechanisms of exercise-induced asthma. Citing an 80% occurrence rate in asthmatic children, he detailed a pattern of initial moderate bronchodilation followed by mild bronchoconstriction after 3-4 minutes of exercise. The major obstruction occurs 2-5 minutes after the cessation of exercise because of bronchial lability. He implicated continuous aerobic exercise of 6-8 minutes as the primary trigger, although severity of exercise also plays a role in inducing bronchospasm. The resultant standard determined for testing and training was intermittent intervals of 5-6 minutes of exercise of 70% maximal capacity with short rest periods interspersed. He also linked exercise-induced asthma to loss of heat and moisture from the respiratory tract. Oseid concluded that interval training for 45-60 minutes at submaximal loads in a humidified, warm environment, following a long warmup of mild intensity would produce the best result with lowest incidence of asthma attack.

Using these testing guidelines, several researchers have evaluated exercise capacity of asthmatic children. Graff-Lonnevig, Bevegard and Eriksson[43] analyzed pulmonary gas exchange during submaximal work. The fourteen males demonstrated higher respiratory rate, lower oxygen and carbon dioxide tensions, and greater alveolar-arterial oxygen saturation at rest. During exercise both alveolar ventilation and minute ventilation increased as in normal references. Metabolic indices were within normal limits. Arterial oxygen and carbon dioxide tension remained low, and alveolar-arterial saturation decreased slightly. The authors suggested that exercise did cause improved ventilation and gas exchange. Thoren[38] has stated that asthmatics develop no changes in the mechanics of breathing. $\dot{V}O_2$ max is reduced only with poor physical fitness. Minute ventilation was greater during exercise to provide adequate gas exchange. He noted a reduction in forced expiratory volume and an elevation in blood lactate during strenuous exercise, and suggested that severely asthmatic individuals have a comparatively larger anaerobic component in exercise.

Few training studies in asthmatic populations exist. Programs for asthmatic children[44] frequently report clinical improvements in height, weight, skill and school attendance. Graff-Lonnevig et al.[45] designed a one year training program for eleven asthmatic boys. He documented changes only in minute ventilation and maximal work capacity. All other changes were not significant if corrected for growth. Clearly, more research in this area is indicated to clarify the outcomes of training in this population.

Another chronic disease of childhood, cystic fibrosis, has been briefly assessed. Godfrey and Mearns[46] noted lower exercise tolerance, lower resting oxygen level and increase in oxygenation with maintenance of end-tidal carbon dioxide tensions during exercise in patients with cystic fibrosis. These values were exacerbated as disease severity progressed. These authors first noted a ventilatory limit to exercise in cystic fibrosis patients. The demonstration by Coates et al.[47] that supplemental oxygen did not increase exercise tolerance further substantiated the idea of limitation from ventilatory mechanics. Orenstein, Henke and Cerny[48] showed that $\dot{V}O_2$ max and peak heart rates were lower in thirty-one cystic fibrosis subjects. Minute ventilation was high for energy output, possibly as a compensation for a large pulmonary dead space. The high correlation between decreased pulmonary function and decreased exercise tolerance encouraged the authors to pose the theory that respiratory muscle fatigue might limit exercise tolerance.

The sweat defect in cystic fibrosis encouraged one group[49] to evaluate exercise in the heat. They noted the thermoregulatory mechanisms to be intact with normal changes in renin, aldosterone and urine salts. Rectal temperature and heart rate were similar in cystic fibrosis subjects and controls. The patients did lose significantly more salt in sweat, so serum chloride dropped severely.

Exercise conditioning has been sporadically evaluated in the cystic fibrosis population. Orenstein, Franklin and Doershuk[50] demonstrated significant improvement in $\dot{V}O_2$ max and exercise tolerance following three months of triweekly training. Training bradycardia was noted in submaximal work. Keens et al.[51] documented increased endurance of respiratory musculature after upper body exercise or specific breathing exercises. Another group[50] has suggested similar effects from a three month running program. One therapeutic project reported by Orenstein, Henke and Cerny in their review article[48] compared traditional chest therapy and bicycling. Preliminary results have indicated equal benefit from each form of exercise, although further research is definitely indicated.

CARDIAC DISEASE

A substantial amount of research has addressed the issues of physical characteristics and exercise potential in children with both congenital and acquired heart disease. DeKnecht and Binkhorst[52] assessed physical characteristics and work capacity of thirty-nine children with both cyanotic and noncyanotic disease. All results noted were more marked for the cyanotic group. Both height and weight were reduced with all subjects below the 50th percentile for fat. Bone age was delayed one year and onset of puberty 3-4 years. Motor development was slowed in both groups with a definite neurological distinction between groups. None of the cyanotic and only three of nine noncyanotic patients had normal $\dot{V}O_2$ max, although all subjects demonstrated a high correlation between $\dot{V}O_2$ and physical work capacity.

Cumming[53] validated the use of the Bruce treadmill test with eight hundred thirty cardiac patients. He stated that the test is valid, but reliability is related to effort. He then documented several interesting relationships. Daily exercise habits correlate directly with exercise capacity, as do height, weight and percent of body fat. Heart rate was not a reliable indicator of maximal capacity in these subjects, so more subjective fatigue was used as an index. The subjects demonstrated elevated oxygen extraction and arterial-venous oxygen difference, suggesting that the cardiovascular system can compensate for an extra cardiac work load. Children with severe valvular disease, cyanotic disease or tetralogy of Fallot were most impaired in physical capacity while those with septal defects or patent ductus areteriosus defects had better abilities. Patients with surgical correction demonstrated normal hemodynamics at rest, but had significant impairment during exercise.

Frick et al.[54] assessed the viability of the exercise pulse as an assessment of cardiac function in fifty-one noncyanotic patients. Only nineteen subjects had a decreased work capacity on a bicycle ergometer. Thus, the author concluded that septal defects are compatible with fitness. Exercise pulse rate was reliable only in cases of gross impairment; pulmonary vascular resistance provided the most sensitive measure.

Direct evaluation of specific cardiovascular and ventilatory responses to exercise in distinct diagnostic categories has been studied by several researchers. Thoren[38] noted that children with atrial septal defects have an abnormally increased respiratory frequency in exercise; reduced work capacity also occurred secondary to a smaller left ventricular stroke volume. Kasch[55] evaluated ten children with ventricular septal defects, pulmonic stenosis and patient ductus arteriosus. All subjects had a decreased $\dot{V}O_2$ max (80% normal for females, 65% normal for males) and a HR max of only 176 beats/minute. Oxygen saturation dropped from 95.8% at rest to 90.8% during step work and was the limiter of exercise capacity. Kasch concluded that these patient groups could participate in normal physical education and less competitive aerobic sports. Epstein et al.[56] assessed atrial septal defect patients following surgical correction. The patients, although asymptomatic at rest, demonstrated reductions in cardiac output, stroke volume, cardiac diameter and cardiac index following exertion. Oxygen saturation remained within normal limits and VO_2 max improved in comparison to presurgical studies. He commented that patients with no symptoms may often have a limited exercise capacity.

Tetrology of Fallot patients have demonstrated a severely reduced aerobic capacity. Low arterial oxygen saturation was one exercise limiter. Low pulmonary blood flow with resultant accumulation of carbon dioxide and secondary respiratory acidosis additionally lowered exercise capacity.[38] Following surgical correction, $\dot{V}O_2$ max increased but was still only 60% normal. Cardiac output normalized, but stroke volume remained low.[38,56] Quattlebaum et al.[57] documented that a small number of patients succumb to fatal arrhythmias, so exercise should be closely monitored.

Children with heart block exhibit varying responses. Ahlborg et al.[58] reported no impairment of exercise capacity in young men with first degree block. Mocellin and Bastania[59] recorded limitation in children with third degree block; maximal cardiac output was only 80% of control values. Children with complete blocks have been noted to demonstrate elevated atrial and ventricular rates during exercise.[38]

Strenuous exercise can be quite dangerous in a few cardiac lesions. Kasch[55] reported that a low physical work capacity secondary to oxygen desaturation in patients with transposition of the great arteries necessitates special physical education activities. Thoren[38] has commented that these patients may also have hidden arrhythmias. Valvular stenosis patients develop abnormal ventricular pressures during exercise with resultant high systolic ventricular blood pressure. Myocardial ischemia was noted after exercise with ST-T wave changes on an electrocardiograph secondary to left ventricular hypertrophy. Recorded systemic blood pressure was low in all cases.[38] Orinius[60] and Maron[61] have reported sudden death from ventricular fibrillation in children with hypertrophic subaortic stenosis. They cautioned against strenuous or unmonitored exercise. Schell[62] has developed guidelines for evaluation of cardiac signs for sports participation. The guidelines clearly define conditions qualifying for safe participation in strenuous versus nonstrenuous activities.

DIABETES

The responses of diabetic children to exercise have been clearly documented by several researchers. Sterky[63] assessed one hundred twenty nine children on submaximal bicycle ergometry. He recorded higher pulse rates in diabetic subjects, but no differences in blood pressure. HR max was greater and $\dot{V}O_2$ max lower in diabetic children, indicating a lower physical work capacity. Deviations in all values were greater with age, leading the author to suggest that lack of fitness rather than the disease process was the causative factor. Thoren[38] noted that prolonged exertion caused no differences in heart rate, blood pressure or body temperature in diabetic children. Utilization of free fatty acids is similar in short-term exercise, but diabetics utilize more carbohydrates in prolonged exertion secondary to an inability to mobilize fats.

Diabetic subjects respond positively to training programs. Larrson[64,65] demonstrated a slight reduction in exercise heart rate, and increase in $\dot{V}O_2$ max and work capacity and a small increase in heart volume in diabetic adolescents following five months of training. Caloric intake increased with no secondary weight gain, while blood sugar decreased. Thoren[38] also cited improvement in blood sugar control with prolonged training. Further research is needed, according to both authors.

BLINDNESS

Relatively little research has addressed the fitness of blind children and adolescents. Seelye[66] administered the Kraus-Weber Test to one hundred eleven visually impaired students in public schools. Results demonstrated that 95% of normally sighted and 85% of partially sighted students passed the test. Only 46% of the legally blind were able to complete the items successfully. The author concluded that lack of participation in regular physical activities was the causative factor. A bicycle ergometer test was used by Sundberg[67] to assess maximal capacity of normally sighted and blind children. Differences in $\dot{V}O_2$ were noted in normal boys and girls, but no sex differences were recorded in blind children. The blind children had significantly lower $\overset{\bullet}{V}O_2$, already established by the age of eight years. The author again concluded that the differences were secondary to different levels of physical activity. Janikowski and Evans[68] described the capacity of institutionalized blind children. $\overset{\bullet}{V}O_2$ max was only 58% of normal values with a concomitant reduction in minute ventilation. Maximal heart rate and tidal volume were also below predicted values. Grip strength was markedly reduced. The author concluded that low endurance of respiratory and extremity musculature was the reason for the deficits.

CONCLUSION

An overview of testing procedures used for assessment of exercise capacity of disabled populations and a brief summary of the physiological findings in these groups has been presented. Clearly, researchers have begun to focus on the evaluation of physical abilities of the disabled. Even more apparent is the need for more extensive work in this area: only the surface has been scratched. A multitude of questions remain to be asked *and* answered. Hopefully, interest and effort will snowball so that more definitive research confirmation of exercise capacity and training effects in special populations will be forthcoming.

REFERENCES

1. McArdle W, Katch F, Katch V: *Exercise Physiology: Energy, Nutrition and Human Performance.* Philadelphia, Lea and Febiger, 1981.
2. Astrand I, Astrand P: Aerobic work performance, a review, in Folinsbee L and associates (eds): *Environment Stress - Individual Human Adaptations.* New York, Academic Press, 1978.
3. Astrand P, Rodahl K: *Textbook of Work Physiology.* New York, McGraw-Hill, 1977.
4. Lamb D: *Physiology of Exercise.* New York, MacMillan Company, 1978.
5. Shepard R: *Human Physiological Work Capacity.* Cambridge, Cambridge University Press, 1978.
6. Davis G, Shepard R, Jackson R: Cardio-respiratory fitness and muscular strength in the lower limb disabled. *Can J Appl Spt Sci* 6: 159-165, 1981.
7. Bar-Or O, Zwiren L: Maximal oxygen consumption test during arm exercise-reliability and validity. *J Appl Physiol* 38: 424-426, 1975.
8. Hulleman K, et al: Spiroergometric and telemetric investigations during the XXI International Stoke-Mandeville Games 1972 in Heidelberg. *Para* 13: 109-123, 1975.
9. Zwiren L, Bar-Or O: Responses to exercise of paraplegics who differ in conditioning level. *Med Sci Sports* 7: 94-98, 1975.
10. Wolf E, Magore A: Orthostatic and ergometric evaluation of cord-injured patients. *Scand J Rehab Med* 8: 93-96, 1976.
11. Hjeltnes N: Oxygen uptake and cardiac output in graded arm exercise in paraplegics with low level spinal lesions. *Scand J Rehab Med* 9: 107-113, 1977.
12. Nilsson S, Staff P, Pruett E: Physical work capacity and the effect of training on subjects with long-standing paraplegia. *Scand J Rehab Med* 7: 51-56, 1975.
13. Glaser R, et al: An exercise test to evaluate fitness for wheelchair activity. *Para* 16: 341-349, 1979.
14. Stoboy H, Rich B, Lee M: Workload and energy expenditure during wheelchair propelling. *Para* 8: 223-230, 1971.
15. Voight E, Bahn D: Metabolism and pulse rate in physically handicapped when propelling a wheelchair up an incline. *Scand J Rehab Med* 1: 101-106, 1969.

16. Brauer R: An Ergometric Analysis of Wheelchairs, doctoral dissertation. University of Illinois, Urbana-Champaign, 1975, cited in: Dreisinger T, Londeree B: Wheelchair exercise: A review. *Para* 20: 20-34, 1982.

17. Knowlton R, Fitzgerald P, Sedlock D: The mechanical efficiency of wheelchair dependent women during wheelchair ergometry. *Can J Appl Sports Sci* 6: 187-190, 1981.

18. Wicks J, et al: The use of multistage exercise testing with wheelchair ergometry and arm cranking in subjects with spinal cord lesions. *Para* 15: 252-261, 1977.

19. Glaser R et al: Physiological responses to maximal effort wheelchair and arm crank ergometry. *J Appl Physiol* 48: 1060-1064, 1980.

20. Glaser R et al: Metabolic and cardiopulmonary responses to wheelchair and bicycle ergometry. *J Appl Physiol* 46: 1056-1070, 1979.

21. Blattgard S, Grimby G, Hook O: Energy expenditure and heart rate in driving a wheelchair ergometer. *Scand J Rehab Med* 2: 143-148, 1972.

22. Glaser R et al: Applied physiology for wheelchair design. *J Appl Physiol* 48: 41-44, 1980.

23. Engle P. Hildebrandt G: Long-term spiro-ergometric studies of paraplegics during the clinical period of rehabilitation. *Para* 11: 105-110, 1973.

24. Dreisinger T: *Wheelchair Ergometry: A Training Study,* doctoral dissertation. University of Missouri, Columbia, 1978, cited in: Dreisinger T, Londeree B: Wheelchair exercise: A review. *Para* 20: 20-34, 1982.

25. Pollock M, et al: Arm pedaling as an endurance training program for the disabled. *Arch Phys Med Rehab* 55: 418-423, 1974.

26. DiCarlo S, Supp M, Taylor H: Effect of arm ergometry training on physical work capacity of individuals with spinal cord injuries. *Phys Ther* 63: 1104-1107, 1983.

27. Gass G, et al: The effects of physical training on high level spinal lesion patients. *Scand J Rehab Med* 12: 61-65, 1980.

28. Molen N: Energy/speed relation of below-knee amputees walking on a motor driven treadmill. *Internat'l Zeit Ange Physiol* 31: 173-195, 1973.

29. Paglierulo M, Waters R, Hislop H: Energy cost of walking of below-knee amputees having no vascular disease. *Phys Ther* 59: 538-543, 1979.

30. Traugh G, Corcoran P, Reyes R: Energy expenditure of ambultion in patients with above-knee amputations. *Arch Phys Med Rehab* 56: 67-71, 1975.

31. Huang C, et al: Amputation: energy cost of ambulation. *Arch Phys Med Rehab* 60: 18-24, 1979.

32. James U: Oxygen uptake and heart rate during prosthetic walking in healthy male unilateral above-knee amputees. *Scan J Rehab Med* 5: 71-80, 1973.

33. James U and Nordgren B: Physical work capacity measured by bicycle ergometry (one leg) and prosthetic treadmill walking in healthy active unilateral above-knee amputees. *Scan J Rehab Med* 5: 81-87, 1973.

34. Bernhardt D: *Comparison of the Physiological Responses of Males with Above-knee Amputations and Normal Males on Arm Crank and Single Leg Ergometry,* 1982, masters thesis. University of North Carolina at Chapel Hill, Chapel Hill, North Carolina.

35. James U: Effect of physical training in healthy male unilateral above-knee amputees. *Scand J Rehab Med* 5: 88-101, 1973.

36. Lundberg A: Maximal aerobic capacity of young people with spastic cerebral palsy. *Dev Med Child Neurol* 20: 205-210, 1978.

37. Lundberg A: Mechanical efficiency in bicycle ergometer work of young adults with cerebral palsy. *Dev Med Child Neurol* 17: 434-439, 1975.

38. Thoren C: Exercise studies in children with chronic diseases, in Berg K, Eriksson B (eds): *Children and Exercise IX.* International Series on Sports Sciences, Baltimore, University Park Press, vol. 10, 1980.

39. Berg K: Adaptation in cerebral palsy of body composition, nutrition and physical working capacity at school age. *Acta Paediatr Scand Suppl* 204, 1970.

40. Lundberg A, Pernow B: The effect of physical training on O_2 utilization and lactate formation in the exercising muscle of adolescents with motor handicaps. *Scand J Clin Lab Invest* 26: 89-96, 1970.

41. Bar-Or O, Inbar O, Spira R: Physiological effects of a sports rehabilitation program on cerebral palsied and post-poliomyelitic adolescents. *Med Sci Sports* 8: 157-161, 1976.

42. Oseid S: Exercise induced asthma - A review, in Berg K, Eriksson B (eds): *Children and Exercise IX.* International Series on Sports Sciences. Baltimore, University Park Press, vol. 10, 1980.

43. Graff-Lonnevig V, Bevegard S, Eriksson B: Pulmonary gas exchange is asthmatic boys during/after exercise, in Berg K, Eriksson B (eds): *Children and Exercise IX*. International Series on Sports Sciences. Baltimore, University Park Press, vol. 10, 1980.

44. Sherr M: Camp Broncho Junction. *Ann Allergy* 28: 428-433, 1970.

45. Graff-Lonnevig V, et al: Effect of a physical education program on the cardiopulmonary function and exercise capacity of boys with bronchial asthma, in Berg K, Eriksson B (eds): *Children and Exercise IX*. International Series on Sports Sciences. Baltimore, University Park Press, vol. 10, 1980.

46. Godfrey S and Mearns M: Pulmonary function and response to exercise in cystic fibrosis. *Arch Dis Child* 46: 144-151, 1971.

47. Coates A, Boyce P, Muller D, et al: The role of nutritional status, airway obstruction, hypoxia and abnormalities in serum lipid composition in limiting exercise tolerance in children with cystic fibrosis. *Acta Paedictr Scand* 69: 353-358, 1980.

48. Orenstein D, Henke K, Cerny F: Exercise and cystic fibrosis. *Phys Sports Med,* 11: 57-63, 1983.

49. Orenstein D, Germann K, Costill D, et al: Exercise in the heat in cystic fibrosis patients. *Med Sci Sports Exer* 13: 91, 1981.

50. Orenstein D, Franklin B, Doershuk C, et al: Exercise conditioning and cardiopulmonary fitness in cystic fibrosis: The effects of a three-month supervised running program. *Chest* 80: 392-398, 1981.

51. Keens T, Krastins I, Wannamaker E, et al: Ventilatory muscle endurance training in normal subjects and patients with cystic fibrosis. *Am Rev Resp Dis* 116: 853-860, 1977.

52. deKnecht S, Binkhorst R: Physical characteristics of children with congenital heart disease: Body characteristics and physical work capacity, in Berg K, Eriksson B (eds): *Children and Exercise IX*. International Series on Sports Sciences. Baltimore, University Park Press, vol. 10, 1980.

53. Cumming G: Maximal exercise capacity of children with heart defects. *Amer J Cardiol* 42: 613-619, 1978.

54. Frick H, et al: The spectrum of cardiac capacity in patients with nonobstructive congenital heart disease. *Amer J Cardiol* 17: 20-26, 1966.

55. Kasch K: Direct $\dot{V}O_2$ max in children with congenital heart disease, in Berg K, Eriksson B (eds): *Children and Exercise IX*. International Series on Sports Sciences. Baltimore, University Park Press, vol. 10, 1980.

56. Epstein S, et al: Hemodynamic abnormalities in response to mild and intense upright exercise following operative correction of ASD and TOF. *Circ* 47: 1065-1075, 1973.

57. Quattlebaum T. et al: Sudden death among post-operative patients with tetratlogy of Fallot: A follow-up study of 243 patients for an average of 12 years. *Circ* 54: 289-293, 1976.

58. Ahlborg B, et al: The significance of AV block 1 ° in asymptomatic young men. *Acta Med Scand* 201.4: 377-380, 1977.

59. Mocellin R, Bastanier R: Functional studies in children and adolescents with congenital complete heart block. *Z Cardiol* 66: 298-302, 1977.

60. Orinius E: Prognosis in hypertrophic obstructive cardiomyopathy. *Acta Med Scand* 206.4: 289-292, 1979.

61. Maron B: Sudden death in patients with hypertrophic cardiomyopathy. *Amer J Cardiol* 41.5: 803-810, 1978.

62. Schell N: Cardiac evaluation for school sports participation. *NY State J Med* 78: 942-943, 1978.

63. Sterky G: Physical work capacity in diabetic school children. *Acta Paediatr* 52: 1-10, 1963.

64. Larrson Y: Functional adaptation to rigorous training and exercise in diabetic and non-diabetic adolescents. *J Appl Physiol* 19: 629-635, 1964.

65. Larrson Y, et al: Physical fitness and influence of training in diabetic adolescent girls. *Diabetes* 11: 109-117, 1962.

66. Seelye W: Physical fitness of blind and visually impaired Detroit public school children. *J Visual Imp Blindness* March 1983: 116-118.

67. Sundberg S: Maximal oxygen uptake in relation to age in blind and normal boys and girls. *Acta Paediatr Scand* 71: 603-608, 1982.

68. Janikowski L and Evans J: The exercise capacity of blind children. *J Visual Imp Blindness* 75: 248-251, 1981.

Handicapped Skiing:
A Current Review
of Downhill Snow Skiing
for the Disabled

David P. McCormick, MD

In recent years the disabled have participated increasingly in sports and recreational activities. Downhill skiing is one of the many sports that have proven adaptable for children and adults with physical handicaps. As of January, 1984, thirty-five clubs across the United States provided recreational skiing and ski racing for disabled persons.[1] These organizations—all members of the National Handicapped Sports and Recreation Association—provide one or more of the following services: adaptive ski equipment, transportation to and from ski areas, individualized instruction, and lift tickets. Many of these services are provided free of charge to disabled participants.

THE HANDICAPPED SKI CLUB

In the Eastern United States one of the most active handicapped skiing clubs is the New England Handicapped Sportsmen's Association (NEHSA). This well organized group has been functioning successfully for ten years and is well known to many disabled sports enthusiasts. It is important to highlight some of the features which contribute to NEHSA's success for individuals wishing to participate in such a club.

NEHSA was founded in 1974 by Fran Rebstad, a lower extremity amputee, when she learned that lessons in amputee skiing were being given by Jim Gardner at Haystack Mt., Vermont. Also involved in NEHSA's founding was Dr. Ben Allen, an orthopedic physician who was a certified amputee ski instructor. Dr. Allen and Mrs. Rebstad moved the club from Haystack Mt. to its present location at Mt. Sunapee in New Hampshire. From these origins the club has grown to a present dues paying membership of about 300, of whom approximately 100 members are disabled.

Dr. McCormick is in practice at Hillside Pediatrics, Baker Avenue, Concord, MA 01742.

That the founders were both amputees was important in providing a focus for the group. Initially the members became expert in skiing for amputees; only later did they expand to provide services for individuals with cerebral palsy, post-polio paralysis, spina bifida and visual impairment. Today, the club still demonstrates its greatest expertise in the area of amputee skiing. Thus, amputees comprise the largest number of disabled members.

One of NEHSA's assets is that disabled and able-bodied members ski together. The disabled athletes see themselves integrating with all who enjoy the sport of skiing. They ride the same lifts, ski the same trails, lunch at the same lodge, and enjoy the same friendships as the non-disabled. All of the club members, disabled and able-bodied, are considered athletes and learn from each other. Differences in ability, need for adaptive equipment, or need for assistance in riding the chair are seen simply as personal differences. In this manner the disabled learn to be understood and accepted for what they can do.

NEHSA is largely a volunteer organization. Many hours each season are donated by ski instructors and NEHSA board members. Although a few paid positions recognize the time commitments and expertise of the equipment manager and the winter program director, funding cannot reimburse all those who donate their time. Members give their time for their love of skiing and their enjoyment in helping others participate. Individuals who have learned to ski reimburse hours of instructor time by becoming instructors themselves. As a result, many of the instructors are themselves disabled. The benefits of this system are obvious; the student learns by identifying with others who have similar disabilities. A two-legged skier cannot really know what it is like to ski on only one leg. The little tricks an amputee learns—how to fall, how to get up from a fall, how to maneuver at the base of the lift, how to handle differing snow conditions and terrain—are often best imparted by someone who is also an amputee.

Another feature of the NEHSA program are the individuals who participate. Their stories capture the imagination of new students: a young man with loss of both feet who wins gold medals in national and international ski championships; a triple amputee who skiis four-track; a blind college graduate; a blind psychologist; a seventy-two year old amputee skier who still skis in Switzerland with her friends. When young people see what can be done it is easy to understand why they participate.

NEHSA benefits from an influx of volunteers from other parts of the United States. Likewise, NEHSA has sent sports enthusiasts to important jobs outside the NEHSA organization. A former NEHSA president is now president of the National Handicapped Sports and Recreation Association; a former NEHSA student and ski instructor is a member of the national instructor's clinic team; a NEHSA member started the handicapped ski program at Okemo Mt. in Vermont. This cross fertilization of ideas continues to stimulate thinking and provides an environment for creative new initiatives in handicapped skiing. For instance, the sit-ski, first developed and used in the west, has now been brought to the east and is being used on slopes in New Hampshire and Massachusetts.

Communications has always been an important aspect of NEHSA's work. Prospective students need to be informed about the program; potential financial resources need to learn about handicapped sports; the public needs to understand what the disabled can do. At the time of the 1983 Winterfest ski tournament NEHSA published a magazine containing articles that describe activities of the organization and its members. Speakers from NEHSA give lectures to many groups, including college departments of physical and occupational therapy and the American College of Sports Medicine. A film describing the NEHSA program is available to interested groups. Videotapes of local and national ski races are shown at ski shows and hospitals. Individuals from NEHSA visit hospitalized patients to dispense information about the NEHSA program. Radio and television spots have been produced; magazine articles and book chapters have been published.[2] An "executive challenge" fundraiser, in which high ranking executives ski-raced in teams with disabled NEHSA members, was held in 1983.

Frequent social gatherings provide the social "glue" for the organization. These include such diverse activities as a "Kickoff Banquet" in December; the Winterfest ski race and banquet; the annual meeting in June; a fund raiser auto rally; summer weekend golf, hiking, canoe, water ski, and camping outings; and shared lunches at the ski lodge on winter weekends.

NEHSA maintains an unusually strong relationship with the State of New Hampshire and one of its state parks, Mt. Sunapee. The state has recently committed funds to make one of its ski lodges more accessible to the disabled. Thousands of dollars were voted for this project by the state legislature. The park authority has been most cooperative in dealing with the special needs of disabled skiers. Lift operators are well-versed in loading and unloading procedures; ski area management is comfortable with the variety of disabled individuals using their slopes. Lift tickets are provided free of charge by the state. This close cooperation and mutual understanding between the disabled and the ski area is essential in the organization of a successful handicapped skiing program.

In addition to free lift tickets, free equipment makes skiing possible for individuals who would otherwise have lacked the financial resources to begin skiing. An equipment trailer provides heated space for boots, poles, outriggers, skis, a workbench, tools and a fitting area. A second heated trailer provides a private changing area for removal and storage of prostheses, and for dressing.

A most important asset is the mountain and its beauty. Mt. Sunapee is located in southern New Hampshire, just a two hour drive from Boston. The mountain's season has been lengthened and improved (with new snowmaking capacities). Seven lifts and 23 trails with a maximum vertical drop of 1,500 ft. provide a variety of experience for beginner to expert skiers. A northerly view from the summit lodge looks out across beautiful Lake Sunapee to the rolling balsam-covered peaks of the White Mountain National Forest. Nature's winter beauty brings people back year after year.

STUDENTS

Students at the NEHSA ski school live primarily in Massachusetts, New Hampshire, Vermont, Maine and Rhode Island. The youngest students range in age from five years. Amputees comprise the largest number of skiers. Some are congenital amputees, or required amputation because of medical conditions in the early neonatal period. Others sustained amputation as a result of accidents or war injuries. Members have lost limbs in motorcycle accidents, or from frost bite and bone cancer.

Other medical conditions of NEHSA members include blindness secondary to retinitis pigmentosa, diabetic retinopathy, congenital cavernous hemangioma, post-polio paralysis, spina bifida, congenital deafness, retrolental fibroplasia, fibromuscular arterial hyperplasia, and cerebral palsy.

ADAPTIVE EQUIPMENT

A variety of adaptive equipment is now available for disabled skiers. Some will ski with two skis and two poles in the usual fashion. Tri-track skiing is popular with unilateral lower extremity amputees who use one ski and two outrigger ski poles. An outrigger is a modified Canadian crutch to which a ski tip or "flip ski" is affixed (Figure 1). Four track skiing is available for the skier with bilateral lower extremity weakness. In the four-track system the skis are commonly held together at the tips with a "ski bra" so the skier can easily maintain the wedge, or snowplow position.

Special adaptive equipment can be custom made as the need arises. A NEHSA four-track skier with a forearm amputation was provided with an adaptive elbow cuff attached to an outrigger (Figure 2). Some students use a stirrup or platform to rest a weak leg or foot (Figure 3). An alternative to the platform is a shock cord tethering the skiless boot to the opposite boot to keep the weak leg from flying out of its neutral position. The "rocker-bottom" ski has been an effective teaching ski. The camber of a ski is the distance between a flat surface and the bottom of the un-

FIGURE 1. The tri-track skier uses a single ski and two outriggers.

weighted ski. A reversed camber or rocker-bottom ski is designed so that the tip and tail of the ski remain in the air when the ski is placed on a flat surface. A reversed camber facilitates ease of turn initiation for beginners. The reversed camber ski is built wider in order to provide a more stable riding surface for the beginning disabled skier.

Cantilevered boot heels are sometimes necessary (Figure 4) for the rare amputee who must ski with a prosthesis. Boot platforms which are hinged and adjustable provide a forward bent-knee stance for ease of turn initiation. The snowmobile has been helpful for lifting students to the top of the beginner's hill when they are not able to climb nor ready to ride the J-bar or chair lift.

Another important innovation in adaptive skiing is the sit-ski, which was first exhibited at the 1980 Winter Olympics for the Disabled. Peter Axelson, a paraplegic who designed the sit-ski, received a silver medal from the British Royal Society of Arts for his design. The sit-ski permits paraplegics and others with weakness or amputation of lower extremities to participate in snow skiing. The sit-skier sits (as in a kayak) with his or her legs covered by a tightly fitting tarp. Steering is affected with a single

FIGURE 2. An adaptive outrigger for a four-track skier with right forearm amputation.

kayak-type ski pole with baskets at each end (Figure 5), or with shortie
ski poles. For safety the sit-ski is tethered to a guide who can slow or steer
the ski with an attached line. Sit-skis are fitted with a low roll bar to protect the skier during a fall; smooth runners enable the skier to skid
through turns. An evacuation device can be deployed in case of chairlift
failure.

A fuller description of the sit-ski and its use is not within the purview of
this article. Further information can be obtained by writing to the Handicapped Ski Program at Winter Park, CO.[3]

SKI SCHOOL

The NEHSA ski school consists of a winter director, ski school director, ski school instructors, volunteers, registration secretary and equipment manager. At the beginning of each ski season instructor's clinics are

held to review teaching methods and sequences for the various handicaps. These clinics begin in the classroom before the snow arrives and progress later to the ski slope.

No student may ski at the ski school without first registering and signing a medical release. Students then have a physical assessment to determine range of motion, strength of muscle groups and muscle tone. Physical therapists or specially trained ski instructors can perform these assessments at the ski area. L. L. Frank, Jr. has published a useful form for listing these functions and for summarizing whether a student's potential for skiing is expected to be good, fair, or poor.[4] The examiner at this time also observes the student's posture, reflexes, gait on a flat surface, and ability to climb stairs. Leg girth and leg length are measured. Leg length is important because some students may require a lift under the

FIGURE 3. This tri-track skier has a weak right leg. A velcro strap across the thighs holds the right leg in place. The right foot rests on a platform.

FIGURE 4. Cantilevered boot shifts the weight forward and allows easier turning for skier wearing lower extremity prosthesis.

FIGURE 5. Kayak-type ski pole helps to steer the sit-ski.

boot. In addition, the following functions are tested: standing balance with eyes open and eyes closed; side sitting to stand; sit ups; push ups; knee bends with reciprocal arm movements; hopping; jumping; half kneeling; heel walking; weight distribution in standing; and toe touch.

Once the physical assessment is completed, the examiner communicates his findings to the equipment manager so the appropriate adaptive equipment can be selected. Bindings are checked for safety release tension. Students are shown how to operate bindings and boots, and how to keep the fingers clear when the bindings are locked into place. The student is checked to see whether he or she is appropriately attired for the prevailing weather. Students are advised to wear a wool cap which covers the ears, wool socks, tucked-in neckerchief or turtle neck shirt, thermal underwear, wool sweater or shirt, ski parka, and thermal mittens (not gloves) padded to protect against falls on the ice. A stump sock, or preferably a stump socket can be worn to protect against the cold and to prevent contusions of the stump when falling on the snow or ice. Such a prosthesis is frequently fitted with a removable peg to provide easy maneuvering at the base of the lift line.

Students skiing with a lower extremity prosthesis should be checked to be sure the prosthesis is appropriately strapped to his or her belt; this prevents the ski from rotating or falling off on the ski lift. In general, students with above-knee unilateral amputations should not ski with the prosthesis as it is heavy and difficult to control. When a prosthesis is worn, accidents can result in a hip injury, stump contusion, or a fracture.

Special lightweight small diameter pegs can be carried attached to an out-rigger while skiing. In this manner the skier can attach the peg whenever he needs to walk a distance. Walking with a peg prevents fatigue and helps to eliminate injuries.

AMPUTEE SKIING

Teaching sequences and techniques have been established for the various disabilities. No comprehensive up to date handicapped ski manual has yet been published. The National Handicapped Sports and Recreation Association intends to publish a manual. Any interested instructor should maintain contact with representatives of this organization. Older publications are either out of print or out of date. Manuals and information on selected aspects of handicapped skiing can be obtained by writing to Winter Park.[3]

It is not within the scope of this article to cover teaching techniques for all disability groups. Since amputee skiers comprise by far the largest group at NEHSA, this technique will be summarized first. The methods described below are similar to those used by Hubbard[5] and Wilson.[6] The teaching sequence takes many principles from the American Teaching Method.[7]

The ski should be a recreational ski of moderate flexibility. It should be no longer than the individual is tall. Skis that are too long contribute to injury.[8] As stated previously, the reversed camber ski has occasionally been helpful for beginners. The boot should be comfortable and of modern design with soft padding and contouring of the boot-top to reduce the likelihood of a boot-top fracture. Outriggers are of several varieties. Many beginning skiers prefer the outrigger with a saw tooth tail to facilitate braking. The outrigger can flip up to provide easy crutch walking.

The progression of steps to skillful amputee skiing is as follows:

1. *Walking:* Initially the beginner can use the outrigger as a crutch with the tips flipped up. Some outriggers flip into a vertical walking position by means of a spring mechanism activated by a cord which attaches near the crutch handle. Walking on the flat, the student can use the outriggers in the horizontal position to push off and glide forward on the single ski. The outriggers initially align at 45 degrees external rotation to the direction of the forward pointing ski. The tip of the outrigger is located at a point even with the heel of the boot. The skier pushes off on the outriggers, drops his knee forward, his shoulders down, and glides along without lifting his ski off the snow.

With some practice the skier can push along on the snow as he smoothly coordinates the thrusts of the outriggers with the actions of leg, body and ski. Walking is good practice and increases the strength of the leg and upper body. The first lessons incorporate much walking. When the leg tires, the student is encouraged to rest by sitting, lying on the snow, or resting in the warming area.

2. *Step around turn:* This turn allows the skier to change direction. The outriggers are oriented at 45 degrees internal rotation with their inner edges planted firmly in the snow. With weight shifted onto the outriggers, the skier hops the tail of the ski in an arc toward the direction he wishes to face while leaving the tip stationary. This maneuver familiarizes the student with unweighting the ski. The student should keep the spine erect to avoid fatigue.

3. *Falling:* All students must learn to fall safely. A student should fall by lowering his buttocks gently down as if he were about to sit on the ski. At the same time the outriggers are thrust forward. As he falls backwards and to the side keeping his stump up and in, the outriggers are lifted up and away from the body (Figure 6). Falling should be practiced in soft snow on the flat until the technique is learned thoroughly. Skillful falling lends confidence, while repeated getting up builds strength.

4. *Getting up:* When getting up on a slope the skier should rotate his body so that the stump is uphill with the ski oriented perpendicular to the fall line (across the slope). Unless this position is maintained, the ski will slide out from under the skier as soon as he stands. The uphill edge of the

c

FIGURE 6. The amputee should fall backwards with the outriggers up and away to avoid being injured by them.

ski should be firmly planted. The uphill outrigger can be used as an aide by planting it upright in the snow near the uphill hip. The uphill hand can grasp the midsection of the outrigger; the other hand can reach over and grasp the top of the outrigger. The body and leg are tucked over the ski. While keeping the nose in front of the knee, the skier pushes with the lower hand on the outrigger, pulls with the upper hand, and stands up.

5. *The sidestep to climb:* A gentle slope is ascended with the ski perpendicular to the fall line. The ski should be downhill with stump uphill. Outriggers and ski are parallel—the uphill outrigger is about 18 inches from the ski—the downhill outrigger is next to the ski. Leading with the hip the skier lifts the ski up and places it down higher on the slope. In this way the skier can climb to a starting place for a straight run.

6. *The straight run:* This is practiced on a gentle slope with a flat outrun which permits the student to come to a natural stop. Outriggers are for balance only and are not weighted, but do maintain contact with the snow about halfway between the boot and the ski tip. Weight is centered over the ski; the body, ankle and leg are flexed in a relaxed position.

7. *The stop:* From a straight run the student can stop by bending down and applying pressure on the tails or brakes of the outriggers causing them to bite into the snow.

8. *The beginning turn:* The student comfortable with a straight run can initiate a turn by steering with the foot and knee. The outriggers are not used for steering but must remain parallel to the ski. When the student can turn in both directions, he can use the chair to ascend the beginners' hill. Some students may need 6-8 hours of lessons before they are ready to ride the chair.

9. *The chair lift:* The student is positioned at the waiting area by the lift operator. When in position the student should look back and sit down on the chair when it is directly behind. Outriggers can be crossed in the student's lap while riding up the lift, but they should be in the ready-to-ski position when the unloading area is reached. Students should keep the ski straight for a direct and fully balanced off-run from the moving lift.

10. *Traverse:* In a traverse the skier moves at a diagonal across the slope. Using gentle slopes at first, the tri-tracker uses the uphill edge to prevent excessive side-slip. When reaching the side of the trail, the skier can turn into the hill to stop, or as an alternative he can steer downhill through the fall line to the opposite traverse.

11. *Side-slip:* While practicing the traverse, the skier can experiment with the side-slip or lateral skid by releasing the edge and sliding laterally on the flat of the ski. The side-slip from a traverse is termed a diagonal side-slip—this maneuver, which gives the student a good feeling for edge control, should be practiced until the student achieves familiarity. The downhill outrigger should be unweighted; the uphill outrigger glides straight beside the ski as in the straight run. The side-slip can also be in-

itiated with a down-up-down movement of the body to release or un-weight the edge of the ski. The upper body should be oriented downhill and the hips toward the hill on these maneuvers.

12. *Uphill christy turn:* This turn allows the skier to turn into the hill and come to a controlled stop. It is the forerunner of all christy turns. The skier's weight comes up, then down, as he skids the tail of the ski down-hill while steering into the slope. The downhill outrigger remains off the snow. The skier should practice this until it is learned both to the right and to the left. Initially, it may be easier for the amputee to turn toward the side of the amputation, but this preference will be overcome with prac-tice. The skier should be able to perform the uphill christy from a position oriented close to the fall line.

13. *Christy turn:* The turn is initiated from a straight run down the fall line beginning on gentle slopes and graduating to more steeply angled pitches. The skier can prepare the turn with a down motion to make a platform for the spring upwards and forwards into the christy turn. Be-ginners should drop their weight down by bending the knee rather than the upper body. The trunk should remain upright as it faces downhill. The advancing skier will learn to link turns as he smoothly passes from one traverse to another. The more expert amputee skier will also learn to turn by initiating a rapid down motion with the body. As the knee flexes, the ski unweights and can be quickly steered in the desired direction. This technique has the advantage of keeping the skier's weight low in a turn, and allowing no loss of contact between the ski and the snow. It therefore provides for a more stable turn.

BLIND SKIING

As various organizations have shown increased interest, downhill and cross country skiing are now available for the blind. The United States Association for Blind Athletes (USABA) has played a pivotal role in organizing such activities.[9] USABA sponsors national and international events. In 1983 a large number of blind ski racers converged at Alta, Utah for championship races. The first international nordic competitions for the blind were held in Norway in 1980, and alpine competitions were held in Switzerland in 1982. In the New England area cross country ski trips for the blind are organized by Ski for Light International[10] and by Blind Outdoor Leisure Development (BOLD).[11] Ronald Salviolo and Michael May have written a new manual for blind skiers entitled *Blind Skiing and Racing.* This manual can be obtained by interested persons for a fee of $10.00.[12] It is published as a bound paperback or can be obtained in braille, audio cassette, Apple Computer discette, and versaBraille cas-sette.

Experienced blind skiers customarily team up with a single ski guide. These pairs ski together for months and sometimes years, often travelling great distances to attend regional, national, or international events. In this way the guide can attain great familiarity with the blind skier's handicap—with familiarity develops a high degree of trust between the two athletes.

NEHSA instructors' clinics have been helpful in providing experience for ski guides. Visual simulators were obtained for use by the NEHSA ski school. The simulator is a pair of goggles not unlike neoprene swim goggles. They are worn over normal eyes to occlude the vision and reproduce the type of visual acuity experienced by students with various forms of blindness. Replaceable lens sets simulate abnormalities such as a narrowed field of vision with or without lens correction, a cataract, a retinal detachment, visual acuities of 20/200, 20/400, or 20/600, and total blindness. One instructor can then guide another whose vision is occluded.

A large variety of guiding systems are available for teaching blind students. On the flat some students prefer holding the instructor's elbow. The instructor should be sure to walk at the student's pace. As an alternative, the student can follow the instructor's clicking ski poles, or can hold the end of the instructor's pole. The instructor should never point the sharp tip toward the student. Another technique is for the guide to ski close behind the student while permitting the student to hold the ends of both the instructor's poles in his hands. A variation of the ski pole technique is the use of two guides, one on either side of the student, who hold a pole between them which the student can grasp with both hands.

The guide must make optimal use of verbal instructions and should maintain a confident tone of voice without shouting and without creating excessive confusion with overly elaborate descriptions.

Blind students are highly attuned to their own bodies and should be instructed clearly relative to use of body parts such as heel, toe, ankle, knee, elbow, spine, head. The blind student can feel the instructor's body to learn some of the positions that can be used in skiing.

Teaching techniques will depend on the degree of visual loss. Students with partial blindness will be able to see the instructor's body as he demonstrates proper positioning and movements in the learning sequence. Partially blind students can follow the instructor's brightly colored bib. Students with total blindness usually ski in front of an instructor who gives verbal commands. At the outset it is important for the instructor to establish the student's degree of visual loss and to determine when the loss occurred. For instance, blind skiers with retinitis pigmentosa may have been losing their vision over a period of years. They may have skied previously, or they may at least have seen skiing. Students with retinitis pigmentosa may also suffer hearing loss which can complicate the process of guiding.

As in all forms of skiing the lessons for blind begin with an equipment review. The instructor demonstrates by touch the names of the parts of the ski—the tips, tails, waist, edges—while describing the purpose of the various parts. The student should become familiar with the workings of the boot and bindings. To foster independence the student should be allowed to put on and fasten his own boot, step into and lock his own bindings. As the student operates the bindings, he should be taught how to avoid pinching the fingers. The design of the ski pole and its proper use should be explained. A large part of the first lesson can be devoted to gaining familiarity with the use of the equipment.

On the flat the blind ski student will learn to glide on the skis and to pole effectively. At this stage it is important for the student to feel the ways in which his leg controls the ski through the boot. As the student pushes the knee down and forward his shin forces against the tongue of the boot-top, and this movement pushes the ski tip down and forward on the snow. The beginning blind skier will often walk by picking up the skis and should be taught to glide. A feel for gliding on the snow can be achieved when the student double poles in Nordic fashion while on the flat snow surface. Walking in a large circle will familiarize the student with the length of the skis. The location of the tips and tails will become increasingly evident as the student is asked to make progressively smaller and smaller circles. Keeping the skis parallel, the student can sidestep partway up the beginner's hill.

Some blind students use the clock face method of orienting themselves with the respect to the hill. For instance, if the skier is standing sideways on the hill with the right side downhill he is at 12:00 o'clock. By turning to 3:00 o'clock he will be facing downhill and will be ready for a straight run.

Selection of terrain for the first straight run is most important. The slope should be gradual enough to avoid excessive speed, but should allow the student to come to a gliding stop of his own accord. The outrun should be free of obstructions such as posts, poles and other skiers. A great deal of time can be profitably spent in such a learning area until the student is comfortable with the required movements, instructions, and positions of beginning skiing.

On the straight run the instructor can guide from behind as he gives commands. The student should maintain good position on the straight run with the knees bent, back erect, hips low, head upright, shins pressed against the boot tongues, skis parallel, arms bent at the elbows, and poles positioned properly with hands somewhat forward of the body as if grasping long motorcycle handlebars. Initially, it may be helpful for the student to ski directly behind the instructor with his hands around the instructor's waist for stability. The student's skis should both be placed inside the instructor's. On a very gradual beginner's slope this technique can provide a controlled method for the student to gain experience gliding down the hill.

At this time the blind student should be taught to fall safely. The student and guide should agree upon a simple command such as "crash," "bail out," or "sit down." On command the student should immediately sit back and down to the side on his bottom. Another command should be used in case the guide falls. On this command the student should come to an immediate emergency stop.

The teaching progression for the blind begins with the gliding wedge. From this maneuver the student progresses to the breaking wedge, the wedge turn, chairlift riding, linked turns and then wide-track parallel turns.[6] While still on the flat the student practices the wedge from the parallel position by pushing the heels to an outward position with the skis flat. This can then be practiced on the beginner's hill as the student creates a gliding wedge by displacing his heels and the tails of the skis outward.

When the gliding wedge is mastered the student can progress to the braking wedge and the wedge stop. Here, the inside edges of the ski are activated against the snow as the student brings his knees together while maintaining the wedge position. The student can brake to a controlled stop as he scrapes the snow away in snowplow fashion. The student should keep the weight forward on the balls of the feet with hands forward to keep himself from falling backwards between his heels while stopping.

The wedge turn is accomplished by steering with the feet and knees while at the same time maintaining the wedge position. The student will learn the wedge turn to stop by turning into the hill from a traverse. The guide should prevent the blind skier from turning too far uphill, or back-sliding will occur. The student should practice steering in both directions using the gliding wedge.

When it is time to use the chairlift the instructor can count down as the chair approaches: " . . . 5,4,3,2,1 . . . sit." The guide should explain the sounds that the student hears as the cable crosses the lift wheels. Guide and student should ski straight off the lift at the top without using the wedge so that the two sets of skis will not cross.

On long gradual slopes the blind skier will learn to link wedge turns. The guide should keep the student in the middle of the trail and keep the skier oriented toward the fall line with constant verbal contact using words such as "turn, turn, turn . . . right . . . turn, turn, turn . . . left . . . turn, turn, hold the turn . . . ". The goal is to provide rhythm and fluidity as the skier gains confidence.

On the slope the blind skier can then learn the standing side-slip with a tail skid as described in the amputee skiing section. Then the skier will incorporate the side-slip into the gliding wedge turn, building into a christy turn. Wide-track parallel turns are accomplished when the student learns to release or unweight the inside ski while performing the turn. Weight is distributed mainly on the downhill ski on the traverse. As the student moves into a wedge and steers downhill the weight shifts to the outside ski as its inner edge carves the turn. Weight is then released from the inside ski (now becoming the uphill ski) which is brought parallel as the skier passes through the fall line.

Some blind skiers achieve remarkable proficiency as they work closely with their guides. Guides who ski ahead of the partially sighted skier should be careful not to get too far ahead and should look back frequently. Quick turns by the edge of the trail should be avoided. A second guide following directly behind the visually impaired student can be available in case of accident.

SAFETY CONSIDERATIONS

Safety is an essential component of any handicapped ski program. A study of handicapped ski racers at the New England Regional Handicapped Ski Championships in 1983 indicates that injuries per skier day are no more common among disabled ski racers than among the able bodied group.[13] Some important steps to safe skiing are:

1. Have bindings lubricated and binding tensions adjusted professionally. Do not change tensions after they have been set.[8,14]
2. Use ski brakes instead of safety straps. The safety strap does not allow the ski to separate from the skier, and the skier can be lacerated by his own ski during a hard fall.[15]
3. Avoid using the wrist strap on ski poles as a fall can result in thumb injury with the wrist strap in place.[16]
4. Cold fatigue sets in after 1-2 hours of skiing.[8,17] Rest in the warming area before a fall occurs.
5. The boot top should be padded and contoured to reduce the probability of a boot top fracture.
6. Avoid ice, moguls, whiteout snow or fog conditions, and excessively steep terrain.
7. Always ski under control.
8. Blind skiers should wear bright bibs to identify themselves.

FITNESS

At the time of the 1983 Eastern Regional races it was found that racers only skied an average of 21 days per ski season. To prepare for skiing and to stay in condition during the ski season the disabled skier should perform regular exercises to increase strength, flexibility and endurance. Slusky published an exercise guide for skiers, much of which can be modified for use by disabled individuals.[18]

The prospective skier can become discouraged if he or she is not physically ready for the strenuous exercise which skiing often demands. Some beginning students are so weak that if they fall in the snow they are unable to get up by themselves—even with much practice. The amputee will require trunk and arm strength as well as leg strength in order to simply regain the upright position once having fallen. Quadriceps strength is particularly important for the amputee skier. Athletes interested in skiing should begin working out even if still receiving chemotherapy. Hospitalized children should have access to physical therapy whenever it is appropriate. A regular exercise program should be a part of any treatment plan and should be tailored to the needs of each patient. Feeling fit correlates well with feeling better.

Some of the ways prospective disabled skiers can improve fitness are as follows:

1. *Trunk.* Knee hug from supine position, bent-knee situp with twist, rocking horse, sitting twist, side bending, upper back lift.
2. *Arms.* Bent leg pushups, shoulder blade squeeze, rotation stretch with towel, triceps stretch, underarm stretch, chair dip, wall pushup, bench pushup.
3. *Legs.* Alternate straight leg raises, wall sitting, bridging, crab walk, step ups, standing hip flexor stretch, thigh stretch, isometric quadriceps contractions, hamstring stretch, prone knee flexion, adductor stretch, chair squeeze, chair spread.

These and many other exercises performed alone or in groups can prepare the athlete for skiing. For those who are able, skipping rope and hopping over obstacles can be a way to increase endurance, aerobic fitness, strength, and coordination. Disabled athletes should avoid these exercises if they cause discomfort in the knee. Swimming, rowing, and pedalling arm-powered cycles or wheel chairs improve aerobic fitness without causing excessive stress on the knee. The athlete should develop a twelve-month fitness program to obtain the optimal benefit.

Physical and occupational therapists should be aware of opportunities for therapeutic recreation. Alpine skiing is now a possibility for individuals with disabilities such as visual loss, deafness, amputation, or paralysis. Many organizations across the country now provide specialized instruction in handicapped skiing. Advances in handicapped ski technique, teaching methods, and adaptive equipment can permit the disabled to ski safely and to experience fully the excitement and beauty of alpine skiing.

BIBLIOGRAPHY

1. For more information write: National Handicapped Sports and Recreation Association, Farragut Station, P.O. Box 33141, Washington, D.C. 20033.

2. Allen A: *Sports for the Handicapped.* New York, Walker and Company, 1981, pp 12-21.

3. For more information write Winter Park Handicap Program, Box 36, Winter Park, CO 80482.

4. Frank LL Jr: Organization and support for a handicapped ski program. *Am J Sports Med* 10:276-284, 1982.

5. Hubbard TK: National Amputee Ski Technique. An unpublished manual prepared for the New England Handicapped Sportsmen's Association instructor's clinics.

6. Wilson S: Manual prepared for the Winter Park Handicap Program. Available from Winter Park (ref. 3).

7. Abraham H: *Teaching Concepts, American Teaching Method,* Boulder, CO: Professional Ski Instructors of America, 1980.

8. Young LR, Oman CM, Crane H, et al.: The etiology of ski injuries: An eight year study of the skier and his equipment, in Eriksson (ed): Symposium on Ski Trauma and Skiing Safety. *Orthop Clin North Am* 7:13-29, 1976.

9. For more information write: United States Association for Blind Athletes, c/o Dick Kapp, 423 W. Grand Ave., Port Washington, WI 53074.

10. For more information write: Ski for Light International, c/o Grethe Winther, P.O. Box 2971, Reston, VA 22091.

11. For more information write: Blind Outdoor Leisure Development, c/o Peter Maines, 533 E. Main St., Aspen, CO 81611.

12. Salviolo RJ, May M: *Blind Alpine Skiing and Racing.* Kirkwood CA, Kirkwood Instruction for Blind Skiers Foundation, 1983. Mailing address: P.O. Box 138, Kirkwood, CA 95643.

13. McCormick DP: Skiing injuries in handicapped ski racers, In press.

14. Hoflin F, van der Linden W: The importance of proper adjustment of safety bindings. In Eriksson (ed) *op. cit.* pp 143-148.

15. Eriksson E, Johnson RJ: The etiology of downhill ski injuries. *Exer Sport Sci Rev* 8:1-17, 1980.

16. Browne EZ, Dunn HK, Snyder CC: Skipole thumb injury. *Plast Reconstr Surg* 58: 19-23, 1976.

17. Westlin NE: Factors contributing to the production of skiing injuries. In Eriksson (ed) *op. cit.* pp 45-49.

18. Slusky TD: *The Skier's Year-Round Exercise Guide,* Briarcliff, NY, Stein and Day Publishers, 1979.

Running for Therapy

Elizabeth Stevenson, EdD, RPT, ACT, CCT

Running is an ancient sport that has had phenomenal growth during the past fifteen years. Current estimates indicate that millions of Americans regularly jog or run. According to Williams et al.,[1] a sizable fraction of this number participate in competitive road racing events that draw in excess of 10,000 participants. Brody classifies levels of performance by the miles run per week.[2] Level one is the fitness jogger or "novice" who runs 3 to 20 miles per week at nine to twelve minutes per mile. Level two is the "sports runner" who runs 20 to 40 miles per week at an eight to ten minute per mile pace and participates in "fun runs" of three to six miles distance. Level three is the "long distance runner" who runs 40 to 70 miles per week at a 7 to 8 minute per mile pace and competes in races of 6.2 to 26.2 miles. Level four is the "elite marathoneer" who runs 70 to 200 miles per week at a pace of 5 to 7 minutes per mile.

The first level or "jogging" has been defined by an osteopathic physician, Perry, as a slow rhythmic step in which the hands and arms are held high and close to the body; the foot strike is short and flat, landing on the heel without any spring.[3] He says that this pattern traumatizes the cervical and lumbar spines. To remedy this, Perry states that in running the arms should be projected anteriorly with the body slanted ten to fifteen degrees forward, eliminating much of the jarring action as the foot then lands in front of the heel near mid-arch and rolls onto the ball of the foot and onto the toes. Bush, another osteopath, also cautions against jogging which he says is too vertical.[4] Bush suggests people should pick up the pace and make sure that the center of gravity is a little ahead of the body to reduce the jarring to the spine. He further states that most people can benefit more by running shorter distances with slanted body than by jogging longer ones. The forward center of gravity in running forces the legs to act as pullers not pushers. Pushing causes one to tire more quickly; hence, Bush concludes that running is less fatiguing and more efficient.

According to Ryan,[5] the National Jogging Association has recognized the major shift of emphasis from the relatively slow-moving, short-stepping activity of jogging to the more physical, long-striding activity of

Dr. Stevenson is associated with the Division of Health and Physical Education, Physical Education Department, California State University, Sacramento, CA.

running by changing its name to the American Running and Fitness Association. They have acknowledged that the pace is the substantial difference between jogging and running. Through the name change they hope to reflect more exactly the interest in development and maintenance of physical fitness.

The purpose of this paper is to review the physiological effects of running in adolescent populations, to present some essentials of conditioning for running in normals, to review briefly the use of running in some disabled populations and to present some alternatives to running.

PHYSIOLOGICAL EFFECTS OF RUNNING

Running has certain obvious advantages. One does not have to have expensive equipment such as skis or rackets; one only needs a good pair of shoes. One does not need a partner with whom to run. One does not have to drive a car to a mountain or a gym. Running has become a family activity with children making up a significant percentage of the entrants in many races. Distances previously thought impossible for the subteens have become routine. From the age of seven there are marathon records.

Any exercise program of an aerobic type, such as running, produces a training effect which, according to Cooper,[6] influences most of the major systems of the body. What are some of the physiologic advantages and disadvantages of this sport for the systems of the body? If the human body is likened to a machine in which every body part contributes to or is affected by the "run" then the three major human networks might be the locomotor, which is composed of the muscular and the skeletal systems, the support network composed of the circulatory, respiratory, digestive and urinary systems, and the regulatory, composed of the nervous and endocrine systems.

Locomotor Network

Musculo-skeletal system: To see the benefits of "use" of the human machine, let us look at some of the negative effects of disuse. Stevenson,[7] after reviewing NASA bedrest and water suspension studies, concluded that deconditioning manifests itself in loss of calcium and phosphorous from the bones and nitrogen from the muscles in a matter of seven days in healthy servicemen. Bed exercises including bicycling did not stop this wasting. This excretion stopped only when weight-bearing and ambulation were resumed. Donatelli[8] described the effects of immobilization on the periarticular connective tissue. He concluded that movement maintains lubrication and critical fiber distance within the matrix to assure an orderly deposition of new collagen fibrils and prevent abnormal cross-link formation.

Does running affect the adolescent musculo-skeletal system in negative ways in growth and development? Epiphyseal injuries have been identified by Pappas,[9] Benton,[10] Rovere et al.,[11] and Wilkins[12] as the weakest link in the musculoskeletal unit for adolescent athletes, but this is less frequent for runners. Some evidence exists that exercise affects growth of the prepuberal child if it is heavy and sustained, but according to Ryan,[13] there is no good evidence that prepuberal children suffer more injuries; he contends that they probably have less than the adult.

Mersereau[14] studied the photographic running patterns of sixty children 2½ to 5½ years of age and concluded that by five years the running pattern of the children resembled that of an adult. Smith[15] did a five year longitudinal photographic study of the running performances of five children and found that as the children grew older they were taller, heavier, ran faster, had a greater stride length, less ground time, and could run further distances. Running was not found hazardous to their health. These were the same conclusions found in Brown's study of thirteen preschoolers, eighteen kindergarteners, 42 second graders and 33 fourth graders.[16]

According to Morehouse,[17] exercise, including running, enables a greater number of muscle fibrils to be activated; causes muscles to become denser and heavier; increases the concentration of sarcoplasmic protein in the muscle; and causes ligaments, tendons and other connective tissues to increase in strength in the adolescent. In addition, chemical changes, such as increased muscle protein and muscle hemoglobin and storage of larger amounts of glycogen, phosphocreatine, and myoglobin, result in the more efficient action of the muscles. Morehouse concludes that exercise for children can increase the thickness of the cartilage at the joint and increase the manufacture of red and white blood cells in the bone marrow. An increase in the number of collaginous fibers produces a thicker and better cartilage to protect young joint surfaces. He maintained that the pressure of running stimulates bone growth up to the optimal length.

Apparently running does not affect the musculo-skeletal system of children in negative ways unless the child is indifferent to the running surface, careless about the type or condition of the shoes used for running, has biomechanical faults in running which may stress ligaments and joints, or has unrecognized congenital problems. These are the same concerns of any runner, regardless of age.

Support Network

If we consider the support network: the circulatory, respiratory, digestive and urinary systems; we are studying the human machine's servicing mechanism for fuel processing and delivery, for oxygen intake and transportation and for waste removal. How does running affect this network in the adolescent runner?

Circulation: The heart becomes larger, slower and more efficient with running in adolescence but, according to Jokl,[18] this is not to be confused with an enlarged heart from critical impairment of its functional capacity nor with a shorter life expectancy. Sady et al.[19] noted that normal resting heart rates were higher in prepubescent boys than in adult men and that their HR increased less with exercise on bicycle ergometers than did that of the adults. This effect of age and exercise on heart rate was validated by Londeree et al.[20] in studying 25,000 subjects from 5-81 years of age on treadmill and bicycle ergometers. They also concluded that young girls have a higher rate than young males. Palgi[21] studied 30 girls and 28 boys (10-14 years) and found that the girls had a significantly higher heart rate. He also found more vasodilitation with a greater peripheral blood flow on running.

Gilliam et al.[22] studied the physical activity patterns of 59 children by recording heart rates before and during an exercise intervention program and concluded that children are not as active as they appear and do not voluntarily engage in high intensity activity. They recommended setting up an exercise trail on school grounds and setting up a large clock with a second hand on the playground to encourage children to run or walk around the school's playground before participating in recess.

Frederickson[23] studied the effects of training on the iron status in the blood of young women cross country runners and found five of the eight young girls had lower than normal hemoglobin. She concluded that iron costs were continually exceeding replacement. Sheehan[24] stated that intensive running can give all the laboratory findings usually associated with anemia (low hemoglobin, fall in hematocrit), but he called this a pseudoanemia. He stated that it is a sign of fitness because, in actuality, the blood volume has increased by about 25%. Sheehan suggested a temporary reduction in training during these periods to allow the body mechanism to regenerate iron. If iron was very low, he suggested taking it orally. Indices of red blood cell (RBC) status were assessed by Puhl et al.[25] on a high school girls' cross country team versus controls. They assessed several times during the running season and found the running group had a higher RBC fragility, supporting the concept of increased RBC destruction rather than hemodilution as the cause.

Francis[26] found a high concentration of high density lipoprotein (HDL) cholesterol in blood of children who ran. He concluded that high levels of HDL cholesterol was a sign of fitness and that it lowered the risk of developing heart disease. The Bassler hypothesis stated that no cases of fatal atherosclerosis have been documented in marathon finishers of any age.[27] The idea that running elevates HDL cholesterol resulting in protection from coronary artery disease is a well publicized theory.

Increasing arterial blood pressure is an important effect of running as it provides the driving force for increasing the flow of blood to and through the muscles. Although moderate running may fail to influence the systolic pressure (the force with which the blood is pumped when the heart is contracting) the pressure rises when the running becomes strenuous. According to Morehouse,[17] it is completely normal for the blood pressure to take longer to return to normal than the heart rate. He found that after a running program the diastolic pressure (blood pressure level when the heart is relaxed) was lower, the systolic pressure increased less during running, and the elasticity of small arteries was increased.

Sutton[28] suggested that thermal injury is the most serious problem facing runners, particularly those that are unconditioned, insufficiently hydrated before running, at extremes of age, overweight or have had a prior heat stroke. Sheehan[29] suggested that it is dangerous to run in the heat at any age, and that to run with an elevated body temperature can precipitate fatal arrythmias. Hughson[30] proposed guidelines using color codes to alert runners to the degree of danger during races and suggested that races should not be started at temperatures above 82 ° F. It would seem prudent for parents or coaches to monitor more closely the temperature in which children run since they are more vulnerable than adults.

In reviewing the literature, Detweiler[31] found that running as an exercise altered blood lipids, increased fibrinolyte activity, promoted collateral circulation, promoted tissue quality of the heart, decreased resting and exercise heart rate, decreased myocardial oxygen uptake, increased blood volume and increased hemoglobin.

In conclusion, a running program has dramatic results on the heart and circulatory system of the adolescent as it does in the adult. After a period of run training, the resting heart rate will be slower and more efficient in pumping blood, the stroke volume will be increased so that fewer heartbeats are required for a given cardiac output, and the heart rate and blood pressure will return more rapidly to normal after activity.

Respiration: There are four basic parts of the respiratory system: (1) lung ventilation or breathing, (2) external respiration where the exchange of oxygen and carbon dioxide occurs between the air sacs of the lungs and the blood, (3) internal respiration where the exchange of oxygen and carbon dioxide occurs between the cell membranes and (4) the respiration within the cells. During running the cells demand more oxygen than they do when resting. With running the increase depends on the intensity and duration of the run. The demand is met by an increase in the rate and in the depth of the respiration.

Much research has identified maximal oxygen uptake as a key factor in human ability to perform physical work. Max $\dot{V}O_2$ determines the maximal capability of the aerobic metabolic processes to deliver energy to the working muscles. Aerobic power refers to the amount of oxygen used (liters or milliliters per kilogram of body weight) per unit of time such as one minute. This usually reflects genetic endowment, ventilatory capacity, capacity for oxygen diffusion, oxygen carrying capacity of the blood, circulatory capacity including capillaries, as well as the musculo-skeletal systems.

In the research laboratory, tests of cardio-respiratory endurance are quite sophisticated. Palgi[21] studied 30 girls and 28 boys (10-14 years of age) using a multistage treadmill, a bicycle task and a 2 kilometer run to determine the relationship between cardio-respiratory endurance and physiological and anthropometric measures. She found the anaerobic capacity to be the most important factor in measurement of endurance in children. Kurowski[32] studied the effect of age on maximal anaerobic power in 294 children (9-15 years of age) and found anaerobic power to be more important than age in determining endurance. The absolute anaerobic power of males aged 9-12 was statistically similar until the age of 13. In females significant increments were apparent after age 10 until age 13, then it leveled off. He also found that young children can increase aerobic power with training. This was substantiated by Massicotte and MacNab[33] in studying 36 boys (11-13 years of age) after six weeks of training on bicycle ergometers.

These studies suggest that running programs affect the respiratory system with slower, more even and deeper respiratory rate, more economical ventilation during work because of an increase in the tidal volume or lung capacity, and a decrease in frequency of respiration. Morehouse[17] suggested that, after training, respiratory rate returned to normal more rapidly, oxygen cost of breathing was reduced, size of capillary bed in the lungs was increased, the number of alveoli used in the exchange process was increased, and a greater amount of oxygen was absorbed per liter of ventilation. He also noted increased respiratory muscle development which enabled more air to be taken in with each breath. Even though each child has a particular capacity for maximum oxygen consumption, training permits him to use this capacity more efficiently.

Digestion: Digestion may be defined as that process whereby food which has been eaten is mechanically and chemically broken down and dissolved so that it may be absorbed into the blood stream. The gastro-intestinal tract includes the mouth for chewing and swallowing; the stomach which is a vat where food is chemically and mechanically reduced; the small intestine where most of the chemical digestion and much of the absorption takes place; the liver and gall bladder where the bile is made and stored, aiding in digestion; and the large intestine which is the storage area for the unusable residue called feces.

The effects of exercise on the digestive system begin in the mouth, causing a decrease in volume and an increase in viscosity of salivary gland secretions. Physical activity of running may retard the emptying of the stomach which is why one should probably not eat solids for two or three hours before running. Rose[34] concluded that anyone who follows a running program should be aware of the potassium depleting capability of this activity and should consume foods high in potassium. He found that money spent on electrolyte supplements is lost unless the ionic concentrations are correct. He determined that depletion of potassium, sodium, magnesium and phosphorus in runners leads to muscle cramps in the leg during exercise.

Cooper and Fair[35] reviewed causes of runner's side ache ("stitch") which they suggest may be from stretching of the large intestine by gas products associated with constipation, local anoxia or spasm of the diaphragm. The pain extending into the upper abdomen along either costal margin is more common on the right side. They recommended relieving the pain by resting in supine position with arms raised above the head and flexing the trunk on the thigh as breath is forced against pursed lips.

Running has little ultimate effect on the digestive process since digestive activity decreases during exercise which, according to Morehouse,[17] is balanced by a subsequent period of increased activity after exercise. He concluded that daily runs appear to improve the motility of the small intestine and promote regularity. In summary, the most important effect of exercise on digestion is probably the diversion of blood flow away from the GI tract. Observation would suggest that running would have a beneficial action on the digestion process because of better muscle tone and circulatory function, enhancing a more active digestive system.

Urinary and Elimination: During running renal function may be characterized by a decrease in renal blood flow to striated and smooth muscles; the degree of this effect depends upon the intensity and the duration of the run. A decreased glomerular filtration rate occurs with the increased sweating rate and reduced renal blood flow, resulting in hypohydration which induces an increase in plasma colloid osmotic pressure. According to the C.I.C. Symposium,[36] there is an increase in filtration fraction, but the reasons for this are unknown. There is a decrease in urine volume and in urine excretion rate. They also reported a decrease in the rate of excreted electrolytes and urinary pH; the presence of proteinurea; and an accentuated urinary appearance of red cells, white cells and epithelial cells. They recommend drinking water which contains approximately the same concentration of NaCl as the sweat being secreted during prolonged exercise in the heat.

The Regulatory Network

The Nervous System: The central (voluntary) nervous system and the autonomic (involuntary) nervous system are the two parts of this system which coordinate and direct all body activity. The ability to run can be affected by poor neural reception, nerve damage, or nerve-ending malfunction of spinal cord and peripheral nerves. During running, an array of electrical and chemical impulses occurs, sending signals to varying muscles to instruct them when and how much tension to produce in the performance of the desired limb movement; to the regulatory parts altering or accommodating to the elevated demands; and to the brain to inform of the complex happenings. In general, we know that a running program facilitates neuromuscular adaptation, which permits highly skilled and coordinated motor performances. Morehouse[17] suggests that, as a result of running, reaction time may be speeded up and we respond to stimuli more rapidly; our kinesthetic sense (sense of perception of movement) may be improved; and there may be a decrease in sympathetic (involuntary, such as sweating) nervous activity. He also reported a reduction in the concentration on a task which is required by the higher centers of the nervous system.

Morgan[37] compares running with drug abuse. He states that the runner who appears in the physician's office on crutches or in a wheelchair as a result of the crippling effects of excessive running is like a hardcore drug addict who has overdosed. Withdrawal symptoms of a neurological nature are evidenced with a layoff. Runners complain of restlessness, insomnia, generalized fatigue, tics, muscle tension, decreased appetite and constipation or irregularity. A true addict, Morgan states, continues to run even when it is contra-indicated medically.

Glandular Control: The endocrine glands located in varying body areas produce important biochemical substances called hormones. They are secreted into the bloodstream and make their way to the cells of the body. If functioning properly, they promote cellular repair and growth. Without them most organic functions, including digestion, would be impaired or would cease. Overweight is considered by many to be a hormonal problem. Exercise effects on overweight are discussed under disabilities in this paper.

Dale et al.[38] studied forty-eight women (16 to 43 years of age) divided into four groups: marathoners, distance runners, athlete controls and sedentary controls. They were evaluated for percentage of body fat composition, cardiac performance during exercise treadmill test, multiple blood chemistry analyses and determination of serum pituitary and ovarian hormone levels. Data from four groups documented the expected decreased body fat of the runners and related this to increased menstrual dysfunction. Serum levels of the hormones regulating menstrual and reproductive patterns were lower in the runners than in the controls.

Lutter and Cushman[39] studied the menstrual patterns of 350 female runners in the 1980 Boston Marathon and the Bonnie Bell 10 km race and found that most of the women (69.4%) continued to menstruate regularly; 19.3% menstruated irregularly with only 3.4% who had not menstruated during the previous year. Sprioff[40] studied running and menstrual function through the use of questionnaires. He found that young women who weighed less that 115 lbs. and who lost more than 10 lbs. after they started running were the most likely to develop menstrual irregularity and amenorrhea. Foreman[41] studied 47 women cross country runners who ran an average of 79.6 miles per week and he found they tended to be irregular. When they reduced their miles per week, they reverted back to normal cycles.

In summary, exercise effects glandular functions, even though some of the changes may be of little consequence in the child's performance either immediately or over a period of time.

SUMMARY

Running is fun. If done with common sense, running is healthful. The average child can expect improvement in the muscular and skeletal systems of the locomotor network, in the circulatory, respiratory, digestive and urinary systems of the support network and in the neural and hormonal systems of the regulatory network.

CONDITIONING FOR RUNNING

Jones[41] and Jensen[42] suggest that research substantiates the great contribution of the warm-up in running. Opinions differ as to the length of the warm-up period, but it is usually about eight to fifteen minutes. Many of the internal physiological adjustments of the body, although automatic, will require a few minutes to be fully set into motion. There also is no agreement as to what exercise to do, but Jensen says it should be intense enough to increase rectal temperature one or two degrees, and should cause perspiration.[42] The gradual acceleration of the heart rate is an indication that a heightened volume of blood has begun to be pumped from the heart. Jensen contends that heat generated within soft tissues of muscles and joints reduces their viscosity and resistance to movement, and improves contractile force and speed.[42]

De Vries[43] suggested that physical work capacity is increased by the greater efficiency of muscle contraction and relaxation secondary to lowered viscous resistance in muscles. De Vries further states that myoglobin and hemoglobin transports more oxygen at higher temperatures. Warm-up increases the metabolic rate of the cell about 13% according to Astrand,[44] in addition to decreasing the resistance of the vascular bed. Jones[41] suggested that neural impulses travel faster at higher temperatures.

The warm-up is generally classified under two categories: the general warm-up involving calisthenics or general body movements unrelated to the specific neuromuscular action of the anticipated performance, and the specific warm-up which provides a skill rehearsal in the actual activity for which the participant is preparing. The warm-up for running could be walking and moving the arms about and then moving into the slow build-up of the specific run pattern.

Greeno[45] has suggested that the training of distance runners falls into three phases: overdistance, interval repetitions and speed training. Overdistance is pushing oneself further than what was attained before. Training adaptation is dependent upon overload or exercise at a higher level of physical activity than usual. Training improvement is directly related to the amount of training with no physiological changes expected until the training stimulus threshold is attained. According to Morehouse,[17] this is approximately 60% to 70% of the maximal heart rate for sedentary individuals and between 85% and 90% of the maximal heart rate for more highly trained persons. Maximal heart rate is estimated easily by 220 minus the age in years. The exercise dosage includes intensity, frequency and duration of effort. The training level should be between 70% and 85% maximal heart rate maintained for 15 to 30 minutes per session three to four days a week.

Detweiler[31] investigated the effect of various frequencies of training on improvement in cardio-vascular endurance of 408 children in the primary grades. He gave instruction in pacing and proper running techniques to 18 classes from the first, second and third grades, and they ran 1, 2, 3 or 4 days per week. He found that the four day a week training group had the greatest cardiovascular improvement of all groups.

Colfer[46] defined interval training as a period of work or exercise followed by a prescribed recovery interval. He used sets for interval training to produce a greater consistency. Each set had a designated number of runs, a designated distance, a timed workout pace and a timed recovery interval. He reduced the workout pace if the pulse exceeded 140 beats/minute. The maximum recovery for any run would not exceed 90 seconds while the minimum would be no less than 30 seconds. He also suggested that the runner keep himself mildly active during the recovery phase. Many authors (Harper,[47] Conley,[48] Butts,[49] and Greeno[45]) have found that interval training with its emphasis on intensity and frequency is more important than the quantity or distance covered. Stocker's parcourse[50] is possibly the ideal for many runners because it is built on the interval training idea of running full speed interspersed with other activities such as a pull-up or push-up at each of twenty stations. Circuit training is an inexpensive but effective method for conditioning young athletes. The circuit can be set up for a large group indoors or outdoors. Hunt[51] adapts a 20 station circuit for varied abilities by having four levels. When a first level student can complete all twenty stations twice in 40 minutes, he moves up to the second level which increases the repetitions and sets, and adds a few exercises.

Speed training is interpreted differently by coaches and may be done as repetition, acceleration or hollow sprints. Usually quick speedy starts are avoided in distance runs but the intensity is gradually increased near the middle and latter stages of the work-out. At any stage of a work-out, if the intensity level of exercise becomes excessive, oxygen and fuel will not be supplied to the highly activated muscles quickly enough to meet their energy demands and fatigue quickly sets in.

It would appear logical that the rate of movement of the legs in sprinting is determined by the length and weight of the legs, the weight of the body, the mechanics of running and the flexibility and strength of the muscles. Flexibility training and weight training have been subjected to much research to determine their contribution to efficient running performance. Evidence in both areas is conflicting. Dintiman,[52] after reviewing the literature, concluded that the combination of both weight training and flexibility training, used as supplements to sprint training, had been shown to increase running speed in the 50 yard dash significantly more than unsupplemented sprint training programs. He recommends static flexibility exercises involving little movement with an attempt made to increase the stride through the use of carefully selected flexibility exercises. A weight-training program involving rapid contractions, high repetitions and light weight should become a part of the sprinter or endurance runner's training.[52]

Plyometric exercise, according to Chu,[53] is another method of conditioning in which the athlete uses the force of gravity to store energy within the body, followed by an equal and opposite reaction using the natural elastic tendencies of the muscles to produce a kinetic energy system. In brief, this means jumping in place, squat hops, and jumping up or down from boxes.

The most important element in evolving a periodization conditioning program, according to Pedemonte,[54] is that the demands of the growing child are considered. Instead of just planning the training program for a season or a year, the program is planned for a series of years including the child's social, psychological and physiological growth.

Because many injuries to runners appear to be caused by bio-mechanical faults, conditioning for running should emphasize the correct foot, leg, and body positioning. Yessis[55] reports that Soviet scientists are developing new technical devices to help automatize control over movements. These devices transmit immediate information to the athlete to facilitate bio-mechanically correct learning. Exercises that use specific elements of the skill or the entire skill as a whole have been designed. These exercises are directly related to the necessary skill and are very specific to the movement required. Electromyography is used to determine how closely the muscle action in the specific exercise duplicates the actual technique. The muscle action in sprinters has been thoroughly studied with subsequent classification of the most effective exercises to approximate running in technique, strength and power. This process is the ultimate in specificity training. Computer analysis of specific muscle function is currently being used at M.I.T. and in Southern California to assist in the training of participants for the 1984 Summer Olympics. According to Potash et al.,[56] this includes a computer, an isokinetic dynamometer, a special interface circuit and a set of programs to perform athletic testing and analysis.

Cooling down after running is just as important as the warm-up. Venous return to the heart is largely supported by the muscle pumps in the legs during running. Sudden cessation of muscle activity may cause blood pooling to occur in the extremities, and thus reduce venous return. A few minutes of walking or light calisthenics allows these muscular pumps to continue working, aids in circulation of the heated blood to the skin cooling centers which, in turn, promotes the body's return to a normal internal temperature level. Stretching muscles and joints facilitates their recovery and counters tightness and soreness precipitated from the lactic acid build-up. The cool-down stretching tasks should be more intense, longer in duration, and more inclusive in number than the warm-up stretches as the elevated body temperature tends to promote elasticity of soft tissues.

RUNNING AND THE DISABLED

Diabetes

Clinicians know that diabetes affects circulation and that insulin requirements are reduced with exercise. Cunningham[57] studied 40 diabetic and 20 non-diabetic volunteer males (18-30 years of age) and found that exercise played a very important role in the control of blood glucose concentration, serving to delay the onset of microvascular deterioration, a complication of diabetes. He found that exercise on a bicycle ergometer enhanced glucose uptake by skeletal muscles. Intense exercise by insulin injected muscles may cause hypoglycemia due to washout of insulin from injection site. Exercise intensity had to be increased 5-7 times the resting metabolic rate to affect blood glucose. He found that cardiovascular adjustments to exercise in asymptomatic well-controlled young diabetics of normal weight can be assumed to be similar to those of non-diabetics. Diabetics could adopt the high-load resistance and endurance training and exhibit the same training effects as non-diabetics. He concluded that endurance exercise in diabetics helps to normalize blood lipid levels, specific clotting factors, and hemoglobin.[57]

Powers[55] stated that the biggest problem facing a diabetic runner is maintaining an adequate blood sugar level during exercise. He suggested a squeeze bottle with 10 teaspoons of sugar, a pinch of salt, a bit of flavoring and 8 oz. of water. Berg[59] discussed how the insulin-dependent diabetic runner can monitor blood sugar levels, insulin dosage, and diet, and complete long distance races. He cautioned that insulin dosage should be decreased if the food intake is not increased the day after competition. Scrupulous care of the feet is necessary in view of the diabetic's predisposition to peripheral vascular disease. Care for the diabetic foot is discussed in detail by Levin.[60] Costill et al.[61] studied ten male juvenile diabetic distance runners and fifteen male non-diabetic distance runners by taking muscle biopsies before, during and after 90 minutes treadmill run at 70% aerobic capacities. They found that to exhibit nearly normal metabolism during running, the diabetic must have some active insulin available to facilitate glucose uptake in muscle. They suggested administering at least part of the daily insulin dose in the evening before the early morning run. Drash[62] stated that exercise such as running increased the efficiency of energy utilization, decreased insulin requirements, and minimized the complications of diabetes in the young diabetic child. Engerbretson stated that regular physical exercise is as important as diet and insulin in the control of diabetes.[63]

Heart Problems

Ignagni[64] collected data on fifteen children with innocent heart murmurs and matched them with fifteen children of the same age and sex who did not have any heart problems. They were assessed on a treadmill for maximal aerobic capacity, heart rate and total endurance. She concluded that healthy children with innocent heart murmurs should not be restricted from participation in running or exercise programs as their cardiovascular systems utilized oxygen as well as the normal children during the maximal exercise test. Rosenthal[65] stated that, in order to relate to their peers, children with congenital heart disease need to exercise to some degree and that most children with congenital heart disease can exercise without restrictions. He recommended that they avoid competitive sports and go for recreational activities such as running.

Rose[66] suggested that any athlete having an unexplained rapid heart rate should not be allowed to participate in competitive sports. He does allow those with T-wave inversions, minor ST elevations, axis deviations, or sinus tachycardia at rest to run. Activity guidelines for young patients with heart disease have been outlined by the American Heart Association[67] and include a chart which could be set up in a clinic. The American Academy of Pediatrics[68] advised that most children with heart problems should be allowed to achieve maximal exertion and should not have restrictions placed upon them.

Overweight

Ross[69] studied the effects of a fitness trail patterned from a parcourse on 14 junior high school girls (13-14 years of age) for eight weeks. The experimental group ran the fitness trail three days a week for a monitored heart rate of 130-180. It was a 478 yard course that the participants ran twice with a different selection of exercises done each time. Ross found that the girls in the experimental group improved significantly in respiratory fitness, anthropometric measures, and reduced waist measures. Brown,[70] Vaccaro,[71] Mayers,[72] Butts,[73] and Rosenthal[65] found a significantly lower body weight and percentage of body fat in runners vs. controls. Distance runners studied by Elrick[74] showed lower than normal body weight, body fat, serum cholesterol and triglycerides and higher HDL cholesterol. The only exceptions were those runners who ate the "average American diet." He concluded that vigorous daily activity for many years does not protect individuals from hypertension and excess body fat or guarantee low serum cholesterol and high HDL cholesterol values if they continue to consume the usual American diet.

Pulmonary Disabilities

In patients with pulmonary disease, exercise can produce functional improvements. Shepherd[75] stated that running increased the mucous flow in pulmonary patients who exercised in a warm, moist environment. The working muscles involved in breathing were strengthened and the anaerobic threshold increased, producing a higher tolerance for normal activities. A training effect resulted in a reduced resting respiratory rate.

Running can be associated with post-exertional asthma in a large number of patients. However, with proper breathing techniques, the asthmatic can learn to handle a running program. If the asthmatic athlete teaches himself to simulate diaphragmatic breathing maneuvers while running, he will do well with a running program. Aronson[76] suggests that exercise-induced asthma can be reduced by control of duration and intensity, proper warm-ups, and by using a surgical mask or face covering that will prevent cold air from reaching the bronchi and triggering a reaction.

Orenstein et al.[77] found that a three months in duration, three days a week walk-jog program conducted at 70% to 85% of each person's peak heart rate increased the endurance of the respiratory muscles in 31 cystic fibrosis patients who represented the entire spectrum of disease severity. Improvement was evident and statistically significant. The exercise group increased peak oxygen capacity and exercise tolerance while the control group did not. The exercise group also developed a training bradycardia with lower heart rates for given submaximal work loads even though pulmonary function did not change. The authors concluded that a walk-jog program may be as beneficial as traditional chest physical therapy and postural drainage for expelling mucous from the lungs, but they recommended that patients continue traditional therapy until this idea is confirmed. Because cystic fibrosis patients lose significantly more salt in their sweat than normal individuals, the authors recommended ample water intake and free access to the salt shaker.

Mental Retardation

Running is one of the basic and earliest forms of locomotion available to mentally retarded children. Jones[78] compared the variation in running patterns from various mental age categories. Data were recorded on film from six subjects with a mean age of 133 months. Two subjects were normal, two were classified as educable mentally retarded, two as trainable mentally retarded, and all were devoid of physical handicaps. She found that those with higher intelligence ran faster, took longer strides and had less of a support phase than did the more retarded children. This does not mean that running does not help all of these children.

Behavioral Disorders

The need for psychotropic medications was reduced in children with behavioral disorders after they began participating in a long distance running program, according to a study completed by Shipman.[79] The 56 children between the ages of 6 and 13 years participated in a voluntary experimental exercise program that had groups of six to ten running a maximum of 40 minutes a day, four days a week for 12 weeks. Kostrubala[80] also found that running had psychological effects which he called "running therapy." He contended that this embodied a fundamental advance in mental health therapy.

Sensorally Inconvenienced

Growing awareness of the benefits of a running program is bettering the lives of many young deaf and blind children. In order to achieve effective mobility in running, these children must have good posture and balance, and running assists in achieving this. The U.S. Association of Blind Athletes (USABA) has its own blind games which include several running competitions. In grade school or high school the blind can run with sighted students and receive all the benefits from this recreation. Trevena[81] suggests that the blind student grasp the sighted student just above the elbow with thumb lateral so that he is positioned approximately a half step behind and a half step to the side of the seeing student. Many high school and college blind students do not need to touch the sighted student at all.

ALTERNATIVES TO RUNNING

Although running can be a great "fixer-upper" of the body and mind, some people cannot run or do not like to run. For them there are alternatives. One such exercise is rebound running. In this exercise individuals jog-bounce on a mini-type trampoline of various dimensions. The energy cost for adults rebound running four days a week ten minutes a day has been determined by Katch et al.[82] They placed it in the moderate exercise category along with walk-jog at 4 to 4.5 mph and recreational swimming.

The opinion of this writer is that, if the study were to be repeated with the subjects alternately bringing the knees up toward the chest (beyond 90° flexion), the authors would find a target pulse rate could be obtained quickly and held for a prescribed period. Although the mini-trampoline reduces stress on knee and on the back, the bio-mechanics of a run in place are important because of possible ankle sprains and pronation of the feet.

In the past few years many Americans have discovered the jump rope as a way to fitness. It doesn't cost much and can be done almost anywhere. It develops cardiovascular fitness, muscular endurance, and improves agility, coordination and muscular strength in the relatively short time of 15 minutes. Kasch[83] suggests a rope of cotton or hemp about 10 feet long, 5/16 to 3/8 inch in diameter, purchased from the hardware store. The amount of rope needed is measured by putting a foot on the center of the rope and pulling the ends up until they reach the armpits. Some people prefer the rope longer so they can hold the arms extended to the side at a 45° angle downward from the shoulder. Kasch reported 15 minutes of rope skipping to be equivalent to an eight mile run. Getchell[83] and Cleary[84] reported that 30 minutes of rope jumping equals 30 minutes of running.

If jumping rope is not appealing, 45 minutes of aerobic dance may be the answer. Simple vigorous dancing takes the place of jogging. Ighanugo and Gutin[85] concluded that the medium and high intensity dance routines provide adequate stress to influence the efficiency of the CV system. Incorrect biomechanics may cause shinsplints, tendinitis, stress fractures and muscle strains in the same manner as in jogging.

Bicycling or, for those less fortunate, stationary bicycling can be used as an alternative to running as it involves the large leg muscles. If the resistance on the bicycle is properly adjusted, riding can elevate the heart rate to the predetermined target and be a good cardiovascular activity.

Bicycling three miles is considered to be equivalent to one mile of running by Dr. Lawrence[86]. Bicycling is not without its injuries, although injuries seem less frequent and less debilitating than running injuries. Biomechanics of the legs, position of the back, and proper height of the seat are all important factors to be considered if one is going to spend many hours bicycling.

Dr. Kenneth Cooper of Dallas stated that running is an excellent exercise but it is not the only type. Many times his patients are restricted to walking. Walking can be a positive approach for patients in rehabilitation programs. They can condition themselves, lose weight and relieve stress without risking musculo-skeletal problems. According to Ryan,[86] walking is gaining favor as an exercise prescription; it is responsible for many times fewer injuries than running as body weight is always supported and the impact of each stride is, therefore, less. Shultz[87] found energy expenditures for walking depend largely on the speed and weight of the walker. He stated that when walking as a fitness exercise or as a conditioning, one must do walking continuously for 15 to 60 minutes carried out at 60% to 90% of maximum heart rate or 50% to 60% of $\dot{V}O_2$ max for three to five days per week.

Dr. Thomas Dawber[86] suggested swimming in cold water as an alternative to running. He stated that there is evidence that by swimming in cold water one hour a day the ability to survive a heart attack becomes even better as the highest energy output is in vigorous activity in cold water. Swimming uses the total musculature and burns up 3,000 calories an hour. Pool exercises to music or cadence, walking or running across the pool, and water games, including water polo for the handicapped, all provide excellent alternatives to running.

Wheelchairs used in track activities and marathons provide an exciting alternative to running for paraplegics and other disabled children. Seven wheelchair paraplegics from a wheelchair basketball team tested the efficiency of having the large wheel at the front versus the large wheel at the back. Mastenbrook[88] determined that the efficiency was greater with the high wheel at the back and that the muscular efficiency values were as great for these athletes as for those running. Higgs[89] analyzed the racing wheelchairs used at the 1980 Olympics for the disabled and found the more successful chairs had lower seats, a seat base at a comparatively higher angle to the horizontal, narrower frames and smaller handrims.

SUMMARY

In conclusion, an effort was made to review some of the literature on the physiological effects of running as it effects the child's three major networks: (1) the locomotor network including the muscular and skeletal systems, (2) the support network with its circulatory, respiratory, digestive and elimination systems, and (3) the regulatory network with the nervous and hormonal systems. Some essentials of conditioning for running were presented, some effects of running in selected disabled populations and some alternatives to running were given for those who cannot run for their therapy.

REFERENCES

1. Williams S, Schocken D, Morey M, et al.: Medical aspects of competitive distance running: Guidelines for community physicians. *Postgrad Med* 70(1), 1980.

2. Brody DM: Running injuries. *CIBA Clin Symp* 32(4), 1980.

3. Monkerud D: Put your health in your hands. *Runner's World Magazine* December, 1980.

4. Bush J: Run properly for workout, coach says. *Physician Sports Med* 4(2), 1976.

5. Ryan AJ: What's happening to running? *Physician Sports Med* 9(10), 1981.

6. Caldwell F: Kenneth Cooper: Preaching the gospel of fitness. *Physician Sports Med* 8(5), 1980.

7. Stevenson E: Deconditioning. Read before the CAPHER Conference, 1974.

8. Donatelli R, Owens-Burkhart H: Effects of immobilization on the extensibility of periarticular connective tissue. *J Orthop Sports Phys Ther* Fall, 1981.

9. Pappas AM: Epiphyseal injuries in sports. *Physician Sports Med* 11(6), 1983.

10. Benton JW: Epiphyseal fracture in sports. *Physician Sports Med* 10(11), 1982.

11. Rovere GD, Gristina AG, Stolzer W: Stalking the vulnerable epiphysis. *Physician Sports Med* 3(7), 1975.

12. Wilkins KE: Youthful bone and muscle. *Emerg Med* March 15, 1979.

13. Ryan AJ: The very young athlete. *Physician Sports Med* 11(3), 1983.

14. Mersereau M: *The Relationship Between Measures of Dynamic Process, Output and Dynamic Stability in the Development of Running and Jumping Patterns of Pre-school Age Females.* dissertation. Purdue University, 1977.

15. Smith SA: *Longitudinal Changes in Stride Length and Stride Rate of Children Running.* thesis. University of Wisconsin-Madison, 1977.

16. Brown EW: *Biomechanical Analysis of the Running Patterns of Girls 3 to 10 Years of Age.* dissertation. University of Oregon, 1978.

17. Morehouse L, Grass L: *Total Fitness in Thirty Minutes a Week.* New York, Pocket Books, 1976.

18. Jokl E: The contribution of sports medicine to clinical cardiology. *Am Corr Ther J* May-June, 1975.

19. Sady SP, Katch VL, Villanacci JF, et al.: Children-adult comparisons of $\dot{V}O_2$ and HR kinetics during submaximum exercise. *Res Quart Exercise Sport* 54(1), 1983.

20. Londeree BR, Moeschberger ML: Effect of age and other factors on maximal heart rate. *Res Quart Exercise Sport* 53(4), 1982.

21. Palgi Y: *Physiological and Anthropometric Factors Underlying Endurance Performance in Boys and Girls.* dissertation. New York, Columbia University, 1980.

22. Gilliam TB, MacConnie SE, Grennen DL, et al.: Exercise programs for children: A way to prevent heart disease. *Physician Sports Med* 10(9), 1982.

23. Frederickson L: *The Effects of Training on the Iron Status of Young Women Cross Country Runners.* thesis. Iowa State University, 1980.

24. Sheehan G: Pseudoanemia: Sign of fitness, not fatigue. *Physician Sports Med* 7(1), 1979.

25. Puhl JL, Runyan WS, Kruse SJ: Erythrocytic changes during training in high school women cross-country runners. *Res Quart Exercise Sport* 52(4), 1981.

26. Francis KT: Sports activities and their effects on high density lipoprotein cholesterol and coronary heart disease. *J Orthop Sports Phys Ther* Fall, 1979.

27. Bassler TJ: Marathon running and immunity to heart disease. *Physician Sports Med* 3(4), 1975.

28. Sutton JR, Bar-Or O: Thermal illness in fun running. *Am Heart J* 100, December 1980.

29. Sheehan G: Be your own stress test. *Physician Sports Med* 5(10), 1977.

30. Hughson RL, Staudt LA, Mackie JM: Monitoring road racing in the heat. *Physician Sports Med* 11(5) 1983.

31. Detweiler GR: *The Effect of Various Training Frequencies on Running Endurance Capacity of Primary Grade Children.* thesis. Old Dominion University, 1977.

32. Kurowski TT: *Anaerobic Power of Children From Ages 9 Through 15.* thesis. Florida State University, 1977.

33. Massicotte DB, MacNab RB: Cardiorespiratory adaptations to training at specific intensities in children. *Med Sci Sports* 6(4), 1981.

34. Rose KD: Warning for millions: Intense exercise can deplete potassium. *Physician Sports Med* 3(5), 1975.

35. Cooper DC, Fair J: Preventing chest and upper abdominal pain associated with exercise. *Physician Sports Med* 6(7), 1977.

36. *Physiology of Fitness Exercise.* CIC Symposium Proceedings. The Athletic Institute, 1972.

37. Morgan WP: Negative addiction in runners. *Physician Sports Med* 7(2), 1979.

38. Dale E, Gerlach DH, Wilhite AL: Menstrual dysfunction in distance runners. *Obstet Gynecol* 54: 47-53, 1979.

39. Lutter JM, Cushman S: Menstrual patterns in female runners. *Physician Sports Med* 10(9), 1980.

40. Bloomberg R: Coach says running affects menstruation. *Physician Sports Med* 5(9), 1977.

41. Jones SS: Enhance performance with warm-up session. *The Winning Edge* 2(4), 1982.

42. Jensen C: Pertinent facts about warm-up. *Athletic J* 56(2), 1975.

43. DeVries H: *The Physiology of Exercise.* Dubuque, Wm Brown & Co, 1966.

44. Astrand PO: *Textbook of Work Physiology.* New York, McGraw-Hill, 1970.

45. Greeno R: Training distance runners. *Athletic J* March, 1974.

46. Colfer GR: Interval training through use of the set system. *Athletic J* February, 1975.

47. Harper DD, Billings CE, Mathews DK: Comparative effects of two physical conditioning programs on cardiovascular fitness in man. *Res Quart* 40(2), 1969.

48. Conley DL, Krahenbuhl GS: Running economy and distance performance of highly trained athletes. *Med Sci Sports Exercise* 2(5), 1980.

49. Butts NK: Physiological profiles of high school female cross country runners. *Res Quart Exercise Sport* 53(1), 1982.

50. Stocker P: Parks get a mile long gymnasium. *Physician Sports Med* 4(1), 1976.

51. Hunt R: An inexpensive but effective method for conditioning young athletes. *National Strength Coach J* January, 1984.

52. Dintiman GB: Increasing running speed through flexibility and weight training. San German, PR, Inter American Univeristy (unpublished).

53. Chu DA: Plyometric exercise. *National Strength Coach J* January, 1984.

54. Pedemonte J: Training the young and intermediate athlete. *National Strength Coach J* January, 1983.

55. Yessis M: The role of specificity in strength training for track, gymnastics and other sports. *National Strength Coach J* Fall, 1982.

56. Potash RJ, Burns SK, Grace P, et al.: Design of a computer based system for isokinetic testing and analysis. *Athletic Training* Summer, 1983.

57. Cunningham LN: *Resting and Exercise Hyperemic Pulsatile Arterial Blood Flow as Related to Endurance Fitness Levels and Duration of Diabetes.* dissertation. Springfield College, 1979.

58. Powers P: Have squeeze bottle, will run, says diabetic. *Physician Sports Med* 7(11), 1979.

59. Berg K: The insulin-dependent diabetic runner. *Physician Sports Med* 7(11), 1979.

60. Levin ME: Saving the diabetic foot. *Med Times* 108(5), 1980.

61. Costill DL, Miller JM, Fink WJ: Energy metabolism in diabetic distance runners. *Physician Sports Med* 8(10), 1980.

62. Drash AL: Managing the child with diabetes mellitus. *Postgrad Med* 63(6), 1978.

63. Engerbretson DL: The diabetic in physical education, recreation and athletics. *JOPER* March, 1977.

64. Ignagni P: *A Comparison Study of the Maximum Aerobic Capacity of Children With and Without Innocent Heart Murmurs.* thesis. University of Wisconsin-LaCrosse, 1979.

65. Moore M: When pediatric cardiology meets exercise physiology. *Physician Sports Med* 10(11), 1982.

66. Rose KD: Which cardiovascular problems should disqualify athletes? *Physician Sports Med* 3(6), 1975.

67. American Heart Association: Council on Cardiovascular Diseases in the Young: Activity guidelines for young patients with heart disease. *Physician Sports Med* 5(8), 1976.

68. American Academy of Pediatrics: Cardiac evaluation for participation in sports. *Physician Sports Med* 7(3), 1978.

69. Ross JW: *The Effects of an 8 Week Fitness Trail Conditioning Program on the Body Image, Fitness Levels of Overfat Adolescent Girls.* thesis. University of Arkansas, 1979.

70. Brown J: *The Development of Prediction Equations on Percent of Body Fat in Three Female Populations.* thesis. Kent State University, 1973.

71. Vaccaro P, Morris AF, Clarke DH: Physiological characteristics of masters female distance runners. *Physician Sports Med* 9(7), 1981.

72. Mayers N, Gutin B: Physiological characteristics of elite prepubescent cross-country runners. *Med Sci Sports* 11(2), 1979.

73. Butts NK: Physiological profiles of high school female cross country runners. *Res Quart Exercise Sport* 53(1), 1982.

74. Elrick H: Distance runners as models of optimal health. *Physician Sports Med* 9(1), 1981.

75. Shepherd RJ: Activity gives psychological boost to pulmonary patients. *Physician Sports Med* 11(2), 1983.

76. Aronson PA: Exercise-induced asthma and the athlete: A review for athletic trainers. *Athletic Training* Summer, 1983.

77. Orenstein DM, Henke KG, Cerney FJ: Exercise and cystic fibrosis. *Physician Sports Med* 11(1), 1983.

78. Jones KC: *A Comparison of the Variation in the Running Patterns of Individuals Selected from Various Mental Age Categories.* thesis. University of Wisconsin-LaCrosse, 1978.

79. Barnes L: Running causes behavior changes in children. *Physician Sports Med* 9(8), 1981.

80. Barnes L: Running therapy: Organized and moving. *Physician Sports Med* 8(6), 1980.

81. Trevena TM: Integration of the sightless student into regular physical activities. *JOHPER* June, 1970.

82. Katch VL, Villanacci JF, Sady SP: Energy cost of rebound running. *Res Quart Exercise Sport* 52(2), 1981.

83. Kasch FW: Rope skipping offers a good aerobic alternative. *Physician Sports Med* 4(4), 1976.

84. Getchell B, Cleary P: The caloric costs of rope skipping and running. *Physician Sports Med* 8(2), 1980.

85. Schuster K: Aerobic dance, a step to fitness. *Physician Sports Med* 7(8), 1979.

86. Ryan A: You can run down running but . . . bikers are hit by cars and swimmers drown. *Physician Sports Med* 3(4), 1975.

87. Schultz P: Walking for rehabilitation: The first step. *Physician Sports Med* 8(10), 1980.

88. Mastenbroek AC: *Delta and Net Muscular Efficiency in Wheelchair Athletes During Steady State Exercise in Two Types of Wheelchairs.* thesis. University of Oregon, 1979.

89. Higgs C: An analysis of racing wheelchairs used at the 1980 Olympic Games for the Disabled. *Res Quart Exercise Sport* 54(3), 1983.

Team Sports

Barney F. LeVeau, PhD, LPT

Team games are important for the child with a disability since they allow the child to be a contributing part of the group. Everyone wants to be a valued team member, but this is especially true for those who are handicapped. Team games can do much to help disabled individuals gain physical fitness and muscular strength, as well as social skills. Disabled children have limited opportunities to be with other children in activities which are mutually enjoyable. Therefore, if at all possible, these children should not be denied the opportunity to be part of a team.[1,2]

This paper will describe some of the needs or motivational drives of the school-age child, some of the anxieties that may be encountered, role of leaders, objectives for team sports in general, objectives for integrating the disabled child into regular team activities, some examples of team sports for the disabled child, and some guidelines for modification of team sports.

NEEDS OR MOTIVATIONAL DRIVES

The disabled child has the same basic needs and motivational drives as other children, which are of major importance in the social growth and maturation of the child. Some of these needs as they relate to participation in team sports will be presented in the following paragraphs.

The physiological need for vigorous activity is essential to organic development and to the total coordinated development of a child.[2,3] Especially in early years, exercise is important, specifically for the proper development of the functional capacity of the heart and lungs, and of strength of bones, muscles, and ligaments.[3,4] To maximize the potential for the child's development, this activity should be available at all stages of the child's life. Few medical problems in childhood should prohibit the child from some type of regular physical activity.[5]

Psychogenic or secondary needs also need to be fulfilled.[6-8] In general these are needs for competence and self-determination.[9] Children have

Dr. LeVeau is Associate Professor, Division of Physical Therapy, Department of Medical Allied Health Professions, University of North Carolina at Chapel Hill.

65

the drive to utilize their full potential, and to be effective in dealing with their environment. The need arouses a tension level in the child which may be reduced by satisfying the need.[8] Some specific psychogenic needs can be met by team sports.

Affiliation, or the need to belong, is one need met as the child seeks and enjoys close and cooperative relationships with other children. The need for achievement or esteem is served as the child rivals and surpasses others, or accomplishes an objective. Many children have the need for aggression and exhibition. They may want to overcome the opposition forcefully, or they may desire to be seen or heard. They want to be on display in a positive manner. Another need is to play as the child attempts to obtain enjoyable relaxation from stress.[7,8]

As a child becomes older, his socialization progresses from individual interests during early preschool years to group activities during the school years.[10] With advancing age the child becomes more social in character and the peer society plays a vital role in the socialization process.[11] Although individual children differ somewhat at the age they become more group oriented, by 10 years most children appear to prefer to use their free time interacting with peers.[11-13] Often this interaction is in the form of spontaneous or organized forms of traditional games. The peer influence is a major motivational factor upon children's formation of standards and in assessing their own performance. The child has the need for affiliation and desires to be accepted as part of the group. The child also needs to achieve, or obtain success within this group.[8]

To be accepted and successful within the peer group, the child must learn the skill of cooperation. Cooperation refers to individuals performing an activity together. It involves a division of labor. Each individual has his special task to perform, as well as a coordination of the tasks. The coordination of tasks or cooperation of several individuals can lead to obtaining specific goals. The result can be a reward for the group, or in some instances, reward for the group and rewards for individuals of the group.[13]

The cooperation of individuals to reach a common goal may infer competition. Competition consists of activities which are directed toward obtaining a standard or achieving a goal where the performance is compared in relation to other selected groups. The peer group should set the standards of performance for individuals within their individual groups; however, adults, as well as peers, set the performance standards for competitive activities in team sports. Group competition can be structured in several ways. It can be developed so that the participants are hostile and aggressive, or so that the participants vie for a reward with friendly interchange. Competitive activities can provide learning opportunities for individuals and groups in such a manner that they are not conducive to destructive conflict, but toward attaining enjoyment, physical activity, a feeling of belonging, and a chance to increase one's abilities. Group competition can be of value for this learning situation since fewer negative social behaviors seem to result from group competition than from competition among individuals.[11] Wise leadership provides opportunities in which all individuals can participate, compete, and have some feeling of success.[13]

Team sports are activities which can afford great opportunities for a child's physical and social development. A team is composed of two or more individuals who are organized to work together for a common cause. When a child becomes part of a team, he meets the need of affiliation. The child learns to work together with others as he performs his specific role within the concept of the team. Depending upon the specific sport, the individual's role may be of major prominence such as a pitcher in baseball, or of less eminence such as the right fielder in Little League. The important aspect is that the child be a contributing member of the team.

As the child fulfills his role on the team, the performance of this role may be evaluated. The child may feel a sense of achievement just by becoming part of the team, but he may feel a greater achievement as he overcomes the opposition, or at least performs his role well. The needs of aggression and exhibition are met as the child challenges the opponent, and as he performs before his peers, and occasionally for his parents and other adults. Depending upon the level of competition, the child can have the opportunity to relax from stresses as he plays the game.[13] Team sports offer various levels of vigorous activity. They can be very physically demanding such as participating in a highly competitive soccer game, or they can be mildly demanding such as playing outfield on a softball team with an excellent pitcher.

ANXIETIES OR FEARS

As the child has basic needs, certain anxieties or fears may also be present. Some of these related to team sports include harmavoidance (avoidance of pain), infavoidance (avoidance of humiliation), and rejection.[6] Anxieties or fears are related to anticipation of danger, or of an unpleasant task or event.[14] Fears tend to be objective and specific, while anxieties are more diffuse and less objective.[8,14] An anxious feeling is often one of being lonely and helpless in a hostile environment.[8] It develops from an uncertainty about the future.[14] Anxiety often is developed as the individual feels a threat to himself or his ego.[5]

Some children have an anxiety over potential of physical harm.[14] They may want to be a member of the team, but they do not want to be put in a situation in which they may sustain bodily injury. In football, for example, a child may avoid making a tackle on a larger player because he is afraid he may be hurt.

Anxiety over loss of love, inability to master the environment, or deviation from expectations may lead to a feeling of humiliation or rejection.[14] Children feel competent if they accomplish their intended goals. If they do not meet the expectations of others, or of themselves, they consider themselves as failures. Early (ages 5-7 years) standards are often set by adults. As the child becomes older the expectations are set more by peers. In adolescence peer standards are of great importance.[14] Children may feel they have lost the love expected by these adults. Their fears seem to be realized if the adults yell at them for missing a thrown ball or failing to make a basket. If a child does not meet the expectations of his peers, he will feel that he has failed.

Two important aspects related to success and failure are based upon: (1) who sets the standards, and (2) the amount of difference between the individual's ability and the value of the standard. The child will feel success or failure in relation to those who have established the standard; whether it was set by adults, his peers, or himself. The degree of success or failure often depends upon the difference between the actual performance and the standard. One may occasionally feel success if he comes close to the standard.[14]

Team sports can provide for many needs of a child, but the basic anxieties must also be considered within this context. Children often enjoy the challenges of tempting danger. Few, however, enjoy the result of injury and pain. Some physical activities can lead to physical harm. Social psychological harm may also occur if the child is humiliated because of a poor performance, or is rejected by the group and not allowed to participate. Motivation may be strong for the individual to participate with the group, but fear or anxiety may overcome the motivation to achieve that goal.[14] The child may find personal adjustment difficult in other aspects of society if he cannot actively participate within the group.[15]

ROLE OF LEADERS

For team sports, high quality leadership is essential. The leadership can set the tone for the level of competition. The level of competition, in turn, establishes several other aspects of the game. Thus, the level of competition is of major importance.

In many instances adults will establish the standards for which the team must achieve success. Many organized team sports for children have national or state championships. To obtain the ultimate success the team must be the champions. The pursuit of this high level of competition does demand a great deal of team cooperation. Each member of the team must perform his task well. This level of competition usually demands a high level of physical activity by the participants within the game and during practices. Under poor leadership this level of competition may, however, introduce several negative factors. The game may no longer become enjoyable. Instead of the sport being a way to release tensions, the game may become the source of tensions. Because of the level of competition, only the best individuals make the team. This takes away for many children the sense of affiliation and is replaced by the feeling of rejection.

This same result along with a feeling of humiliation occurs if the child makes the team, but does not play in the games. If the player does play, he may make some sort of mistake which could lead to the loss of a game. The child then may be humiliated in front of his peers by his coach, parents, and peers. The high level of competition may also lead to injury. Each child is striving to do his best. Often over-exertion, over-aggressiveness, or purposeful attack of the opponent can bring about an injury to the child or his opponent. When a team competes in an organization which provides a high level of competition the results can be very harmful to the child's development. Only a few participants obtain the ultimate goal.

This result, even in highly competitive team sports, need not occur. With proper leadership and guidance the team members may learn how to be part of a team, to win and to lose, and to have fun even at the highly competitive level. In competitive situations winning is important, but the definition of "winning" may be different for different people. Some examples include the strikers soccer team and the dunkers basketball team.

The strikers soccer team which had an average season was entered into the final tournament of the year which included teams from within and outside of the state. The age groups were separated into two divisions. The best six teams in one division (A) and the remaining six teams in the other (B). The strikers were placed in the B division. During the tournament they were undefeated and not scored. Although they had played in the B division, the team members were elated because many of their needs were met.

The dunkers, an average basketball team, were playing the second ranked team in the state. The score was close for the entire game. Only within the final minute of play did the highly ranked team outscore the dunkers to win the game. Even though the dunkers lost the game, the team players all were overjoyed because the team had done so well.

Winning or losing a specific game is not always the most important factor. The important factors are that the players did their best and played fairly. The coaches, parents, and peers must recognize these factors as the measure for success in team sports.

GENERAL OBJECTIVES

Team sports organized by adults should meet certain objectives based upon the needs of the children. These objectives should be that:

1. Every child if at all able should be on a team and play a sufficient amount of each game.

This objective can be met when the leaders assure that everyone "signing up" to be on a team is placed on a team. The leaders should attempt to make the teams of somewhat equal ability. The coaches should insure that each team member participates in each game. Because of some coaches' zeal to win, some children may be allowed to play in the game for only a brief time. Organizations may have to make and enforce rules, which require coaches to put their substitutes into the game. For example, instead of having only nine baseball batters bat before the first batter's turn arrives again, all team members must bat before a player bats a second time. The score keepers can "keep track of" all players who have participated in the field. Every player should play at least one inning in the field.

Basketball can be monitored easily as well. Each team could be assigned only ten players. Each player must play at least one half of two quarters of the game. The participation may be controlled by having five players play for half the time in the first and third quarters and the other five team members play the other one-half of the time in the first and third quarters. If each quarter is 6 minutes in duration, at the end of three minutes the referee will stop the game and have mandatory substitution. For the second and fourth quarter the coach may substitute the team members as he desires.

2. Every child should obtain some feeling of success.

How does a child really feel success? Lack of rejection and humiliation, and reaching a certain goal provide measures of success. The leadership can help the child gain success by setting realistic goals. To win the game is the most obvious measure of success. Leaders may help provide each team with potential for success by assigning players to each team so that the teams are similar in ability. The coaches should teach skills and strategy to every player so that the skill level of each player and of the team improves. Sometimes only little things bring success to a child. Scoring one basket in a basketball game may be enough. Getting to bat or fielding a ball in baseball may be sufficient. Making a good tackle in soccer or football may provide success for some children. A positive approach to these situations by the coach, the parents, and peers may be all that is needed for the child to believe that he had achieved something.

3. Every child should gain a degree of fitness and enjoyment from the activity.

For a child to gain physical fitness from a sport he must participate. The physical fitness obtained does relate to each individual's level of fitness. A child with a high level of fitness may gain only very little. The components of fitness gained may also vary depending upon the intensity level of the specific sport. The intensity level of most sports may be adjusted and is often determined by the competition. Not all sports increase one's cardiovascular fitness, muscle strength, or flexibility. Coordination, balance, and skill, however, may be gained as the child participates in games and well organized practices. Appropriate coaching procedures, rules of the game, and enforcement of the rules should be maintained to prevent injuries. If injuries do occur proper first aid attention should be available.

The activity should be administered so that the child will enjoy the activity with minimal stress. Some stressful situations can be of value, but the overall goal should be to limit the number and duration of these situations. Shooting a free shot or being up to bat can be stressful. Missing the shot or striking out may be even more stressful if that result is overemphasized. The attitude of the coach, parents, and teammates controls the stress and enjoyment of the activity. If the attitude is that the child participate, tries to do his best, and enjoys the game, the child will have a positive, enjoyable experience from being a member of a team.

Ideally the disabled child should participate on a regular team without, or with the fewest possible, adaptations of the equipment, facilities, or rules. Games should play according to the basic rules whenever possible.

When allowing integrated participation for the disabled child in regular team activities several factors must be considered. The leader of the activity should take into account the following points.

1. The child should be able to perform all the skills adequately. This means that the child does not have to be the "star" of the team, but should have sufficient skills to allow him to perform as well as many of the other team members. Some team sports will allow for a less skilled or fit player to participate in a position that will hurt the team less if a mistake is made.
2. The child should be able to perform the skills and participate on the team safely. The child should not be at any more risk than any other participant. The participation by the child should also present no additional risk to the other players. The team activity should not aggravate any existing injury. To prevent problems which may occur, the coach must keep a watchful eye on the players. He should also communicate with the child's parents and physician to gain knowledge

about the child's medical background. The leader should be aware
that overzealous parents, however, may not mention or may not
realize the potential dangers.
3. An error or mistake in the child's performance should not unduly
   reflect upon the handicapping condition and cause social or psychological problems related to the condition. Even the best player on the
   team makes an occasional mistake. When a player including one
   with a disability makes a mistake, the leader of the group should not
   place great emphasis on the error. Encouragement for the child to
   improve is the better approach. Correct instruction would benefit
   the individual.
4. The level of competition of the activity may influence whether the
   child with a disability should participate. A program that is recreational in character would have less pressure upon winning than a
   program that progresses to major championships.

The decision for the individual child to participate in regular team
sports should be based upon his abilities, not upon his disabilities.
Children with similar disabilities may not have the same abilities. One individual may successfully and safely participate on a team, even a highly
competitive one, while another individual with a similar disability may
not. The decision must be made on an individual basis.

Children with disabilities often can participate on regular teams. The
following represents only a few. Children with cardiac problems can participate in team sports as their condition permits as indicated by a physician. Children with mild or moderate levels of cardiac problems may become team members in low competitive games such as being baseman in
softball, setter in volleyball, play line position in football, or playing goal
keeper in soccer or hockey. The leader of the activities must always obtain guidance from the child's physician. The final choices of participation for the individual depends upon the leadership and the individual
himself. The child must be able to meet the challenge of regular team
sports by having sufficient skill, strength, and emotional abilities to participate.

Deaf children participate individually or on teams within recreation
and school leagues. A deaf child can play in most team sports including
basketball, baseball, volleyball, and soccer. The team, however, must
work out signals which prevent possible injury resulting from the child's
inability to hear warnings of danger.[16,17]

Children who are blind in only one eye may have little problems participating in regular team sports. Partially seeing children have had some
success playing football, soccer and basketball. Softball and baseball may
present problems for the partially seeing child as the ball is hit or thrown
rapidly in his direction, or to his blind side.[17]

If certain conditions such as epilepsy, asthma, and diabetes are under control, a child with one of these problems may have little difficulty, participating in the regular program. For example, a high school student with epilepsy can be ''All-Conference'' in football; a teenager with asthma can play goal keeper, or maybe limited time in the field in soccer; and a child with diabetes may do well in softball.[1,18]

Individuals with amputations have participated adequately in several team sports. A person with bilateral upper limb amputations can play soccer with minimal balance problems, but cannot throw the ball in from the sidelines. A child with a single upper limb amputation may be able to play most team sports including baseball. Bilateral lower limb amputations may limit participation; children with single limb amputation however, would be capable of playing softball, baseball, basketball, and volleyball. Playing regular football, soccer, and hockey would probably be restricted for these individuals.[17]

MODIFICATION OF TEAM SPORTS

Rules, equipment, or facilities may be modified in various ways. This section presents only a limited guide for the modification of team sports. Several books have done this in some detail,[2,10,12,17-19] Following, however, are some examples of modifications which can be made. No set method for modification of activities exists. The modifications within the guidelines previously presented are only limited by the imagination.

A child with a disability may not be physically able to participate on a regular team. These children should not, however, be deprived of playing on a team. For the child with a disability to play team sports, often some part of the sport must be adapted or changed. The modification or adjustment of an activity may be made in the rules, equipment, or facilities.

Any modifications of team sport should meet the needs, interests, and abilities of each player. They should follow certain guidelines.

1. The modification should be based upon a physician's medical diagnosis. Children with several different problems may be included on the same team. The modification must be designed so that the child's condition is not further aggravated. Constant evaluation of the modifications need to be made to ensure the positive effect of the modification.
2. The modification should be made so that the child with a disability will be able to have success. The adaptation should fit within the ability and skill level of the child. As the abilities of the players improve, the modification may be changed to provide further challenge to the participant's abilities.
3. The modification should be realistic in relation to the child's age and

interests. The modification should not be perceived by the child as being too easy or below his or her dignity.

4. The modification should provide for safety of the players. None of the adaptations of the facilities, equipment, or rules should present hazardous conditions to any of the team participants.

General

— Allow children in wheelchairs and crutches to substitute these forms of locomotion for running.
— Have the players walk instead of run.
— Vary the speed of the activity.
— Increase the number of players on the team.
— Hold the hand of a blind child while he is running.
— Shorten the playing time.
— Use heavy balloons for balls.
— Put a bell in the ball for blind children.
— Make smaller field or court dimensions.

Baseball or Softball

— Use a batting tee instead of a pitcher.
— Use arch in pitch as in slowpitch softball.
— Have an adult pitch.
— Do not have strike outs or walks.
— Shorten the pitching distance.
— Provide a designated runner for the batter.
— Allow the fielder to stop and kick the ball with his feet.

Basketball

— Lower the baskets.
— Shorten the free shot line.
— Liberalize the dribbling rules.
— Use of wheelchair.

Football

— Use flag or tag instead of tackling.
— Change blocking rules by disallowing leaving the feet in blocking.

Soccer

— Reduce the size of the field.
— Eliminate running with stationary soccer on a small field.
— Reduce the goal size.
— Change the ball size.

Volleyball

— Use a throw as a serve.
— Allow catching and throwing of the ball.
— Eliminate rapid motion with stationary play.
— Lower the net.
— Increase the allowable number of times hit.
— Allow lower limb hits.
— Have blind players as designated servers.

SUMMARY

Children have many needs and drives which need to be met. This is also true for the child with a disability. These needs include affiliation, success, aggression, exhibition, and physical fitness needs which can be met by participation in team sports.

If at all possible the child with a disability should participate with other children on the regular team without modification of the game. In some instances the child will not be capable of participating on a regular team. Rules, equipment, and facilities of sports, however, can be modified for team members so that they will be able to play team games. One of the most important aspects of providing team sports is the knowledge, attitude, and creativity of the leaders.

REFERENCES

1. Mathews DK, Kruse R, Shaw V: *The Science of Physical Education for Handicapped Children.* New York, Harper and Brothers, 1962.
2. Vannier M: *Physical Activities for the Handicapped.* Englewood Cliffs, NJ, Prentice-Hall, 1977.
3. Gordon IJ: *Human Development.* New York, Harper and Row, 1962.
4. Cumming GR: Medical comment in sport and physical activity, in Albinson JG, Andrew GE (eds.): *The Child in Sport and Physical Activity.* Baltimore, University Park Press, 1976, pp 67-77.
5. Epstein S: The self-concept: A review and proposal of an integrated theory of personality, in Staub E (ed): *Personality: Basic Aspects and Current Research.* Englewood Cliffs, NJ, Prentice-Hall, 1980, pp 81-132.
6. Alderman RB: *Psychological Behavior in Sport.* Philadelphia, WB Saunders, 1974.
7. Krech D, Crutchfield RS: *Elements of Psychology.* New York, Alfred A Knopf, 1958.
8. Schultz D: *Theories of Personality.* Monterey, CA, Brooks/Cole Publishing Co, 1976.
9. Deci EL: Intrinsic motivation and personality, in Staub E (ed): *Personality: Basic Aspects and Current Research.* Englewood Cliffs, NJ, Prentice-Hall, 1980, pp 35-80.
10. Miller AG, Sullivan JV: *Teaching Physical Activities to Impaired Youth: An Approach to Mainstreaming.* New York, John Wiley and Sons, 1983.
11. Fait HF: *Special Physical Education: Adapted, Corrective, Developmental,* ed 4. Philadelphia, WB Saunders, 1978.
12. Johnson RC, Medinnus GR: *Child Psychology: Behavior and Development.* New York, John Wiley and Sons, 1965.
13. Sherif CW, Rattray GD: Psychosocial development and activity in middle childhood (5-12 years) in Albinson JG, Andrew GE (eds): *The Child in Sport and Physical Activity.* Baltimore, University Park Press, 1976, pp 97-132.

14. Mussen PH, Conger JJ, Kagan J: *Child Development and Personality,* ed 3. New York, Harper and Row, 1969.

15. Arnheim DD, Auxter D, Crowe WC: *Principles and Methods of Adapted Physical Education.* St. Louis, CV Mosby, 1969.

16. Clarke HH, Clarke DH: *Developmental and Adapted Physical Education.* Englewood Cliffs, NJ, Prentice-Hall, 1963.

17. Guttman, L: *Textbook of Sport for the Disabled.* Oxford, Alden Press, 1976.

18. Masters LF, Mori AA, Lange EK: *Adapted Physical Education.* Rockville, MD, Aspen Systems Corporation, 1983, pp 229-236.

19. Sherril C: *Adapted Physical Education and Recreation,* ed 2. Dubuque, IA, Wm C Brown Co, 1981.

The Competitive Spirit

Donna B. Bernhardt, MS, RPT, ATC

Competitiveness has become a cultural value in American society. Individuals compete on all levels of life experience—mental, emotional and physical. Metaphorically, life is a "rat race"; the "battle" of the sexes looms large; we "run" around like madmen to keep up. Our language suggests a rivalry or contest. While the origins of this competitive behavior are unclear, its ubiquity in our culture suggests a degree of inherence in human nature. Competition is possibly a fusion of the need to achieve and the desire to compare oneself to others.[1]

While many promote competition as normal and healthy, some evidence suggests that it increases antisocial and reduces presocial behavior, especially in the developing child. Social games and play provide situations important for socialization and identity formation. Games provide a safe, time-limited situation in which to test oneself, to simulate principles of social interaction, and to gather information about one's abilities. Stringent organization of sport frequently negates these potential values.

Competition is defined by Webster as "effective opposition in a contest."[2] If appropriately planned, competition can incorporate the educational principles of shaping, reinforcement, gradual assimilation, and development of coping mechanisms. These skills are important to every child, but especially to the disabled child who might have more limited social dialogue.

This article presents a survey of regional, national and international events of a competitive nature. These programs hopefully provide an arena of positive competition for many disabled individuals, permitting development and expansion of their social personality.

NATIONAL EVENTS

Organized competitive sport for the physically disabled was born shortly after World War II when disabled veterans began forming basketball teams at various Veterans Administration hospitals. The first national

Donna B. Bernhardt is Assistant Professor, Boston University, Sargent College of Allied Health Professions, University Road, Boston, MA 02215.

"tour" occurred in 1948 when the Long Beach "Flying Wheels" competed against other veteran teams across the United States. The developing interest spawned the first National Wheelchair Basketball Tournament at the University of Illinois in 1949. A National Wheelchair Basketball Association (NWBA) was formed in the same year. This association governs the one hundred sixty-eight national teams that are organized into twenty-seven conferences. The NWBA has adapted NCAA rules for all competitive events. Regional and sectional playoffs occur each spring, culminating in a national tournament. National teams are chosen by the NWBA for international competition. In addition, the association has recently established intercollegiate and women's basketball competition.

Following the lead of several European countries, Benjamin Lipton, Director of the Bulova School of Watchmaking, guided the development of the first National Wheelchair Games in New York in 1957. These games, patterned after the Stoke-Mandeville competition in England, had very few competitors the first year, but rapidly grew once knowledge of the competition expanded to other disabled persons. The need for organization and regulation of a wheelchair sports program quickly became apparent. To this end, the National Wheelchair Athletic Association (NWAA) was founded in 1958. The overall governing body is the National Wheelchair Athletic Committee which formulates rules and regulations, maintains athletic records, selects national meet sites, and chooses international representatives.

The National Games, held yearly in June, are an enormous event. State and thirteen regional qualifying meets are held in the spring for over twenty-five thousand competitors. Predetermined performance standards must be met in order to qualify for the national games. All entrants undergo evaluation by physicians and physical therapists to determine level of muscular function for competition classification. Classes IA to IC are quadriplegic levels, while classes II and VI are paraplegic or comparable disability levels. Participants with amputation(s) are placed in class IV to VI dependent on location and level of limb ablation.

Seven events are included in the National Games: track, field, swimming, weightlifting, archery, table tennis and a pentathlon. Track events include the slalom, a race against time on a course defined by flags and complicated by ramps and platforms, and the dash (60-1600 meter lengths). Javelin, shot put, discus and club throw are the permissible field events. The swimming strokes allowed in competition are the breast, back and front freestyle, butterfly, individual and distance freestyle. Lengths of swim races vary from 25-400 yards. The sole event in weightlifting is the bench press. Division is determined solely by body weight. Archery competition involves accuracy from various distances. Table tennis events allow both singles and doubles competition. The pentathlon embraces all track and field events.

Several other sports have developed on competitive levels for persons in wheelchairs. The National Wheelchair Softball Association governs and coordinates softball competition, using adaptations of official softball rules. Competition culminates in a national softball tourney in late spring. Wheelchair tennis against able-bodied or disabled opponents is regulated by the National Foundation of Wheelchair Tennis. Rules are similar except two bounces are permissible before the ball is declared dead. A national championship closes yearly competitive play. Both the American Wheelchair Bowling Association and the NWAA offer competitive bowling, governed by American Bowling Congress rules. Ten to sixteen pound rubber or plastic balls are allowed, as are wrist aids and ball carrier clamps. League and regional tournament play culminates in a six day national tournament.

Wheelchair competition is ever-enlarging to include many other sporting events. Road racing is coordinated by the Wheelchair Road Racers Club. Both horseback riding and wheelchair football are growing in the direction of competitive organization. The near future will probably include development of these and other sports for wheelchair competitors.

Paralleling this development of wheelchair competition, sports for the ambulatory disabled have been emerging. In the 1970's separate meets were sprouting across the United States for persons with cerebral palsy and allied disorders who were not eligible for existing handicapped sports associations. To this end, in 1978, the United Cerebral Palsy Association formed a branch, the National Association of Sports for Cerebral Palsy (NASCP). The national office coordinates production of educational and promotional materials, provides technical assistance in the area of sports development, serves as liaison to other sports organizations, and facilitates programming and competitions. Representatives of six national districts make recommendations on any portion of the sports program. Ad hoc committees are developed to address specialized issues.

NASCP has developed a separate classification system to address athletes with cerebral palsy or brain damage with motor dysfunction. Participants are classified by a NASCP certified physician or physical therapist based on demonstrated proficiency in a battery of functional tests. Classes I to IV are wheelchair classifications for both quadriplegic, triplegic, hemiplegic or paraplegic participants. Classes V to VIII are for ambulatory quadriplegics, hemiplegics, paraplegics or triplegics.

The sanctioned events in all competitions include archery, horseback riding, powerlifting, table tennis, wheelchair and ambulant soccer, bocci, bowling, rifle shooting, and track and field events. Local and regional meets are held yearly. A National Soccer Meet is held yearly, but the National Meet for all other events is held in every odd-numbered year. In all even-numbered years, an international meet is sponsored. The international meet is held simultaneously with the Olympiad for the Disabled every four years. Athletes for both national and international competition are selected by the NASCP Advisory Board.

Another association, the National Handicapped Sports and Recreation Association (NHSRA) was formed to address solely ambulatory sports, especially for those with amputations. This organization with regional branches governs ambulatory competitions in several sports, primarily alpine and cross-country skiing. Concurrent with the formation of this association, ski programs for the disabled have been developing. The oldest and largest program is established at Winter Park, Colorado. The program began at Arapahoe Ski Basin as a ski training program for amputees in 1968. Personnel changes necessitated a move to Winter Park in 1970. The program currently teaches skiing seven days per week to persons with over fifty different disabilities. An accessible housing area, Zephyr Village, is also available to skiers who remain for several days of instruction.

In other parts of the country similar smaller ski programs have developed to provide both instruction and skiing experience to the ambulatory disabled. These programs are organized either by a particular ski area or by a local branch of the NHSRA. During the ten-week ski season, various local ski competitions are held, culminating in regional meets in February of each year. Regional champions then compete in a national competition held in March, coordinated by NHSRA and the Winter Park Program. Participants are classified by location or level of amputation(s), by level of functional disability and by method of skiing (two, tri or four track; ski pole alteration; use of guide; or pulk). Events include slalom, giant slalom and downhill for all competitors. International teams are chosen by NHSRA from the national winners.

The Special Olympics were initiated in 1968 at Soldiers Field, Chicago as a competition for persons with mental retardation and physical disability. A Special Olympics Committee oversees all state organizations. Each state coordinates local and county meets. Every county has a competitor quota for each event, and sends these competitors to sectional and state competitions. Classification is based on age and ability (qualifying score). All competitors must be at least eight years of age. Volunteer coaches train the competitors for any of sixteen official events: track and field, swimming and diving, gymnastics, basketball, soccer, volleyball, softball, field hockey, alpine and cross country skiing, bowling, speed and figure skating, frisbee, and wheelchair disk and slalom. Many states also offer non-official events, including cycling, equestrian events, senior sports and integrated able-bodied/disabled team sports. The culmination of the meets is an international winter and summer Olympics held every four years.

Since 1979, the National Kidney Foundation has spearheaded the development of sports and competition for patients who have had renal transplants. Classification for all events is by age and sex. Each participant must present a certified medical release form and a medical history before becoming eligible for competition. The authorized competitive events are table tennis, tennis, badminton, squash, golf, swimming and track and field. Accepted swimming strokes are the breaststroke, backstroke and freestyle in 50 and 100 meter heats. Track and field events include 100, 400 and 1500 meter dashes; minimarathon; 400 meter relay race; ball throwing; shot put and high jump. The addition of volleyball and windsurfing will occur in 1984. The competitive season involves state and five regional meets, culminating in an International Transplant Olympics. The most outstanding athletes, chosen by the National Advisory Board, comprise the fifty member United States team to this international event.

Ski for Light was organized as a program of cross-country skiing or ski touring for visually impaired and physically handicapped persons. The National Ski for Light organization governs and coordinates several regional divisions. The program is primarily instructional with a guide/instructor for each participant. Each region organizes clinics and weekend trips for members to provide skill development and ski touring experience. A week long International Ski for Light event is held yearly for participants from the United States, Canada, Norway and other countries with similar programs. Cross country races are conducted on the final day for any participants who are interested.

One self-competitive activity of note is the Outward Bound program. Based on the motto "I have learned that there are no limits to my efforts, unless I limit myself," Outward Bound provides self-discovery and outdoor skill development in seven regional schools without ceilings. Two courses of fourteen days duration have been developed for the hearing impaired and the physically disabled. Both courses admit disabled and able-bodied participants in a shared self-discovery. The courses, held at the Minnesota school in the summer, develop skills in canoeing, portaging, night paddling, white water navigation and rock climbing.

INTERNATIONAL EVENTS

The first international sporting event for persons with physical disabilities occurred in 1952 at Stoke-Mandeville Hospital, England. The primary event was archery competition with only England and the Netherlands competing. The success of this event led to the addition of more events and more competitors. The Games, formally recognized by the International Olympic Committee since 1956, are held annually in England. Since 1960, the Games have been held in the hosting country of the regular Olympics prior to Olympic competition in every fourth year.

These games have been nicknamed "The Parolympics." Sports for the disabled truly emerged in 1976 when the First Olympiad for the Physically Disabled was held in Toronto, Canada. More than fifteen hundred athletes from thirty-eight countries participated. Classification for competition in the games is based on disability level. Two categories exist for the blind, twelve for those with amputations and six for all neurologic and paralytic disorders. Assignment of classification is accomplished by an internationally certified team of physicians. The Games are subdivided into wheelchair, blind and amputee games. Events common to all groups are swimming, track, field and pentathlon. Wheelchair competition also includes archery, weightlifting, fencing, table tennis, rifle shooting, snooker, slalom and basketball. The blind games incorporate bowling, goal ball, wrestling and skiing. Games for amputees allow table tennis, rifle shooting, bowls, football kicking, slalom, volleyball and skiing. Rules and regulations as decreed by the International Olympic Committee are used with minimal modification when necessary.

Following the lead of the Stoke-Mandeville Games, the Pan American Paraplegic Games were established in 1967, encouraging competition between North and South American countries only. The European, Far Eastern and South Pacific Games soon followed. All these games use rules, classification system and event structure similar to the Parolympic Games. All are held biannually.

Another international event has developed as recently as 1976. Called the Winter Olympics for the Disabled, it was held in France in 1976 and in Norway in 1980. Very few countries and competitors were represented in 1976, but by 1980 over two thousand disabled athletes from eighteen countries attended. Athletes include those with amputations, visual limitation or paraplegia. Classification by disability level is decided by physician/physical therapist teams from the represented countries. Four classes exist for amputees, two for the blind and four for paraplegics. Athletes are also divided by sex, age and ability. Events for amputees include alpine (giant slalom and slalom) and cross-country skiing. The blind compete only in cross country skiing, while paraplegic events include bobsled racing, pulk skiing and ice picking. The United States was requested to bring an exhibition team in 1980, composed of disabled persons for whom no classification level or event existed. Included on the team were a double above-knee amputee, a polio patient with one flail lower limb, a girl with unilateral proximal focal femoral deficiency and blind skiers who competed in alpine events. The hope was to change and modernize the current classification system to encompass more disability groups.

In addition to the Winter Olympics, a World Disabled Ski Championship is held yearly with the exception of the Olympic year. Thirty nations compete in events similar to the Winter Olympics. The United States Team amassed more medals in 1982 than any other country.

As previously mentioned, the Special Olympics hold an international winter and summer event every four years. These events are staggered so that either a winter or a summer olympic competition is held every two years. Unlike the disabled international events, the Special Olympics is the only one not based on ability. Use of the quota system allows both superior and average athletes to compete against others of similar age and ability.

CONCLUSIONS

A broad spectrum of national and international events has been reviewed. The constant development of more competitive events for an enlarging pool of disabled individuals is a very positive symbol for the world of disabled athletics. The disabled are discovering the same physical, emotional and mental benefits from sport as able-bodied competitors. These competitions not only serve as a positive factor for the competitors but perhaps more importantly, increase public awareness and education. Outstanding athletic performance is understood by everyone. It speaks to capability louder and clearer than a thousand words.

REFERENCES

1. Burke E, Kleiber D: Psychological and physical implications of highly competitive sports for children, in Straub W (ed): *An Analysis of Athletic Behavior,* edition 2. New York, Movement Publications, 1978.

2. *Webster's New World Dictionary of the American Language,* Second College Edition. New York, The World Publishing Company, 1970.

Body Image and Physical Activity

John M. Silva III, PhD
Jennifer Klatsky

A common belief is that participation in appropriate physical activity programs can aid in the development, improvement, and maintenance of a variety of physiological, psychological and social aspects of the individual. Some avid proponents of the psychological benefits of physical activity have maintained that exercise can have a notable effect upon self concept, self esteem, personality, confidence, body image, and social adjustment. While systematic and well controlled research in each of these areas has not been totally convincing, an accumulation of material suggests that physical exercise can influence body image, self concept and subsequent behavioral change. Many practicing health professionals have experienced the problems generated when a client has poor self concept and body image. Foremost among these problems is a noncooperative attitude or outright abstinence from physical activities related to the rehabilitation process. Such an attitude may slow the recovery process and, in some instances, prevent a patient from experiencing full recovery from physically debilitating operations or injury.

Body image represents an important component in the overall self concept possessed by an individual. Schilder has provided one of the earliest and widely accepted definitions of body image indicating that it is the reflection or picture an individual has of his or her body and the qualitative self identity attached to this perception.[1] Once this image is formed, is it lasting and resistant to reinterpretation? The question of whether participation in physical activity can improve body image has been asked for decades and is still a concern for contemporary health professionals involved in physical activity or rehabilitation programs. Many health professionals find themselves working with individuals who perceive their bodies as ineffective, inadequate, and generally an aesthetic embarrassment. Removing a feeling of physical incompetence through physical activities often represents a significant alteration in not only one's attitude toward the physical self but also in one's attitude toward one's total self

---

Dr. Silva is an Assistant Professor, Department of Physical Education, University of North Carolina at Chapel Hill. Jennifer Klatsky is a PhD Candidate in Counseling Psychology, School of Education, University of California, Berkeley.

image. In order to facilitate such a difficult process, health professionals should be aware of the most effective techniques that can potentially provide participants with physical change and the concomitant enhancement of psychological wellbeing.

In this paper the authors will examine the relationship between participation in physical activity and body image. Two of the major issues in this analysis relate to the development of body image and to the factors that influence the malleability of body image.

BODY IMAGE AS A PSYCHOSOCIAL PHENOMENON

In the broadest sense, body image encompasses the general perception and evaluation of one's physical and motoric self. Schilder emphasized that cultural and social forces help shape an individual's conception of body image.[1] Clearly, the "body beautiful" for the female gender has been operationally defined in terms as diverse as the endomorphic shapes evident in nineteenth century art; the ectomorphic figure exemplified by the 1960's model Twiggy; and the mesomorphic-athletic profile propagated in the 1980's. As with the ideal female body, the ideal male morphology has been characterized by variations between the ectomorphic shape[2] and the mesomorphic V shape.[3] While cultural-social forces clearly influence the conceptualization of body image, other forces of input play extremely important developmental roles. Hunt and Weber, for example, note that sensory and perceptual experiences influence the development of body image.[4] Piaget maintained that the individual begins to develop body image by attending to body parts and organizing body perception very early in life.[5] Infants discover and experiment with different body parts by seeing and moving them. This visual-manipulative process plays a major role in the child's acquisition of knowledge about the body and the consequent development of body image.

Much social learning during early childhood deals with the management of bodily functions and the acquisition of culturally-based attitudes toward the body and body parts. Body size and the child's image of his or her own size may be of particular significance in social interactions between the child and peers, parents, and other adults.[6] Perceptions of body parts and their functional abilities, the relationship of one's body in space, and the ability to regulate movement in space all provide valuable feedback about the image one has of one's body. When this feedback is interpreted as evidence of incompetence, feelings of inferiority may develop. This psychological reaction has been found to be especially common in young children and adolescents who find themselves in a social environment that places physical appearance and prowess at a premium.[7]

As indicated by Fisher and Cleveland, the term body image ultimately describes a unique subjective evaluation that may operate in both an idealized form and realized form.[8] Thus, body image is a dynamic conceptualization that one is and at the same time reacts to. If body image is in fact a dynamic concept, we should turn our attention to the question of changeability. A basic tenet existent in many health professions is that, through intervention, enhancement of physical, social, and psychological wellbeing can be achieved. Can body image be changed through movement experiences?

MALLEABILITY OF THE BODY IMAGE

Schilder has suggested that the development of body image is continuous throughout life and can change as the result of new or powerful experiences.[1] Physical changes in body weight, strength, fitness, skill, or ability, as well as changes due to accident or illness may all result in consequent changes in body image. Stunkard and Mendelsohn's studies of obese patients with body image disturbances (in the form of extreme preoccupation with obesity) showed that body image improvement (due to long-term psychotherapy) tended to occur prior to weight loss and actually was a favorable prognostic sign for weight loss success.[9] Simmel's observations of amputee patients showed that the body image appears to be established early in life.[10] Children younger than four years old rarely experienced phantom digits and limbs after amputation, while children aged eight years and older often experienced phantoms. Simmel concluded that experience and memory of previous sensory input from the limb was necessary in order to create phantoms after amputation. Simmel additionally observed adult leprosy and amputee patients and found an absence of phantom experiences for those digits which were reabsorbed gradually over a period of several years.[10] This absence was explained as being a function of the slow, progressive nature of the loss. Apparently the body image can keep in step with physical reality via small, gradual changes which parallel the physical alterations of the body. Under these conditions one is less likely to experience a phantom limb response. When, however, sudden alteration of physical reality resulting from an acute amputation or alteration occurs, the body image cannot keep up and phantoms are experienced or body image remains unchanged.

Glucksman and Hirsch also found evidence supporting the early development and "fixing" of the body image with adult subjects who had been obese since childhood.[11] These individuals lost approximately 85 pounds over the course of eight months and were found to manifest a "phantom body size" phenomenon. The subjects actually perceived their bodies as if they had lost virtually no weight. This phantom was maintained throughout the eight month period of weight loss and continued after an additional year of weight loss. The authors hypothesized, as did Simmel,[10] that the physical alterations in body configuration occurred more rapidly than could appropriate alterations in the psychological perception or attitude toward the body image. These studies tend to indicate that, in order for a change in body image to be maximized, the change must be gradual and accompanied by attitudinal and behavioral changes. That is, bodily shape change should be accompanied by a modification in self perceptions of one's physical self, and this attitudinal change should be manifested behaviorally through new activity patterns.

A person's attitude toward body image can have behavioral implications that reach into adulthood. Kagan and Moss conducted a longitudinal study and found that children who possessed high degrees of fearfulness about their bodies demonstrated similar amounts of somatic fearfulness as adults.[12] This early anxiety also appeared to have effects upon the individual's long-term behavior. Boys who held high body anxiety tended to avoid athletic activities and pursued more solitary, intellectually-oriented activities in later years. Thus, negative body image may suppress the opportunity for engagement in physical activities. This avoidance strategy reduces the likelihood that the individual will experience the very environment that could positively modify his or her body image over time. While such a strategy may provide some degree of psychological protection, little productive activity transpires that could modify the very nature of the body image problem. The avoidance of physical activities by individuals with poor body image is unfortunate since some research exists that supports the idea that a variety of movement experiences can contribute to the development of positive body image.[13] Movement can alter perceptions of bodily movement capacities and can also lead to a better body-environment orientation. We do not know very much about our bodies unless we move them. By movement we come into definite relation to the outside world—its constraints and liberties. Only in relation to the outside world are we able to correlate diverse impressions concerning the capacities of our bodies. Evidence suggesting that a reduction in movement is related to the distortion of body image has been presented by Kreitler in his studies of aging adults.[14] Individuals over fifty years old who seldom engaged in movement tended to have a more distorted image of their bodies. These individuals often perceived their bodies to be broader and heavier than they actually were and when compared to active older individuals exhibited greater distortion of general body image. As the distortion of image increased, participation in physical activities was perceived as more difficult. Thus, as previously mentioned, a closed loop system develops in which body movement becomes infrequent, body image becomes more distorted and perceptions of physical competence are lowered leading to decreased desire to engage in movement activities.

Harris suggested that this cycle may also be in effect in younger indi-

viduals and children who have had limited or unsatisfactory experiences
with physical activity.

> Children who do not have satisfying and varied movement ex-
> periences during childhood may develop a distortion of body image
> which will influence their participation in physical activity the rest
> of their lives. By the time they get into organized classes of physical
> education, this distortion is such a part of them that they do not find
> physical activity pleasing and will resort to almost anything to avoid
> it. Distortion of body image creates bodily insecurity and lessens the
> desire for physical activities.[13] (p 146)

Intervention by health professionals might be successfully accomplished by providing a program of physical activity which counter-acts
the development of the body image distortion. The acceptance of one's
present bodily characteristics without excessive self judgement is extremely important and perhaps a precondition necessary before an individual can commit to a program of physical movement or activity that
will require both time and effort.

STRUCTURING A PROGRAM

Read's research suggested that physical activity programs could be structured to enhance body image by ensuring that each participating individual enjoys a certain amount of success. In his study of the influence of
competitive and noncompetitive physical education programs, those individuals who were constantly successful had significantly higher positive
body image and self concept scores than did those who were constantly
failing.[15] Apparently keeping physical activities within the range of all
individuals may have the important effect of maintaining or improving the
body and self images of *all* participants. If competition is introduced into
an activity program designed to rehabilitate or improve body image, caution and careful planning are required. Otherwise, individuals who could
potentially benefit the most from these programs may drop out following
early failure to perform or keep up. Such feedback would serve to reinforce existing attitudes that define one's bodily capacities and body image
as undesirable.

Harris, for example, found that men who have been active throughout
their lives and consider themselves to be athletic enjoy being watched by
others, want to compete, keep score and desire to win. They are generally
more confident of their movement and of their ability to perform in
physical activities than are their less active peers. Harris suggested that
these findings indicate that a sense of successful participation in physical

activity promotes a desirable body image, or that those individuals who are secure with their body image are more inclined to participate in physical activities.[16]

If the promotion of positive body image is a goal of a rehabilitation program, then activities must be structured in a manner that insures some degree of participant adherence. This point is crucial since, as reviewed earlier, changes in body image occur slowly over time. When adherence to structured activity programs has been accomplished, several studies have been able to demonstrate positive change in body image and self concept. Collingwood and Willett found significant increases in positive body attitude, self attitude, and self acceptance, as well as in physical fitness performance, in obese teenaged males after they participated in a physical training program.[17] Collingwood found similar results in a group of male rehabilitation clients who participated in a physical training program. These subjects demonstrated significant increases over a matched control group in physical fitness performance, and positive physical, intellectual, and interpersonal behaviors.[18] Hilyer and Mitchell found students low in self concept experienced significant positive changes as a function of engaging in a program of running and flexibility training. In addition, subjects who received the physical training plus counseling designed to emphasize the relationship between movement and self concept evidenced positive change that surpasses the physical training alone and control groups.[19] This program demonstrated that *physical* and *attitudinal* change provides the strongest prescription for modification in perceptions of body image and self concept. The authors note that increased physical efficiency of a noticeable magnitude makes it easier for a clinician or health professional to reinforce initial attitude modification demonstrated by the subject. The physical and psychological domains reinforce each other in a manner that can effectively modify a subject's self perception. Additionally, activities such as running and flexibility training are excellent modalities since each provide the subject with an increased sense of mastery and control over the self. Decreasing running time, increasing distances covered, or experiencing a greater range of movement via improved flexibility all contribute built-in, tangible rewards to the participant who maintains involvement.

Thus, programs of movement and physical activity can be structured in a manner that promotes change in self concept and body image perceptions. While this is encouraging, these programs require regular participation in activities that are often strenuous and generally require several weeks of commitment. Body image change is a slow process requiring not only a physical change but also attitudinal and behavioral modifications. With this caution in mind, practitioners interested in implementing systematic programs designed to modify body image are offered the following guidelines:

1. Initiate body image change programs with a careful interview of each subject.
2. Determine the attitudinal and physical concerns that must be addressed by the clinician. Are particular body parts (e.g., stomach, thighs) or bodily functions (e.g., aerobic capacity, strength) primarily responsible for poor body image perceptions?
3. Establish clear objectives for yourself that are quantifiable. This will allow you to document any positive or negative change.
4. Have clients contract to a period of time that will allow for physical, attitudinal and behavioral change to occur (6-8 weeks minimum). Establish written improvement goals for the contract period in each of the three areas.
5. Select activities with built-in rewards such as walking, running, flexibility or strength programs. As previously mentioned strength gain or increases in distance are tangible rewards that can be self motivating to the client.
6. Have participants engage in group exercise but avoid one-on-one competition that focuses upon outcome. Keep participants process oriented and aware of progress toward their individualized goals. Social interaction can promote adherence to an activity program, however, clients should not become dependent upon others in order to be active.
7. Continually provide feedback that can facilitate attitudinal change that includes self acceptance, a desire for a healthy lifestyle and functional use of various bodily parts.
8. Avoid unrealistic goals or desires that relate to an idealized view of body image. Such a perception ultimately leads to failure, frustration and a regression of self perceptions.

By having a systematic plan, body image change can occur in a rehabilitation setting. Whether treating children, athletes or the infirm, experiencing such change can be extremely rewarding for both the client and the clinician.

REFERENCES

1. Schilder P: *The Image and Appearance of the Human Body.* New York, Wiley and Sons, 1950.
2. Staffieri RJ: A study of social stereotype of body image in children. *Personality and Social Psychol* 7: 101-104, 1967.
3. Darden E: Masculinity-femininity body rankings by males and females. *Psychology* 80: 205-212, 1972.
4. Hunt VV, Weber ME: Body image projective test. *Projective Technol* 24: 4-10, 1960.
5. Piaget, J: *The Construction of Reality in the Child.* New York, Basic Books, 1954
6. Katcher A, Levin MM: Children's conceptions of body size. *Child Dev* 26: 103-110, 1955.

7. Cratty BJ: Psychology and Physical Activity. Englewood Cliffs, NJ, Prentice-Hall Inc, 1968.

8. Fisher S, Cleveland SE: *Body Image and Personality.* Princeton, NJ, Van Nostrand, 1958.

9. Stunkard A, Mendelsohn M: Disturbances in body image of obese persons. *Am Dietetic Assoc* 38: 328-331, 1961.

10. Simmel ML: Developmental aspects of the body scheme. *Health and Social behav* 8: 60-64, 1967.

11. Glucksman ML, Hirsch J: The response of obese patients to weight reduction: The perception of body size. *Psychosom Med* 31: 1-7, 1969.

12. Kagan J, Moss HA: *Birth to Maturity: A Study in Psychological Development.* New York, Wiley and Sons, 1962.

13. Harris DV: *Involvement in Sport: A Somatopsychic Rationale for Physical Acitivity.* Philadelphia, Lea & Febiger, 1973.

14. Dreitler H: Movement and aging: A psychological approach. *Physical Activity and Aging.* New York, Karger, Basel, 1970.

15. Read DA: The influence of competitive and noncompetitive programs of physical education on body image and self concept. Unpublished Doctoral dissertation, Boston University, School of Education, 1968.

16. Harris DV: Physical activity history and attitudes of middle-aged men. *Medicine and Science in Sports* 2: 203-208, 1970.

17. Collingwood TR, Willett L: The effects of physical training upon self concept and body attitude. *J Clin Psychol* 27: 411-412, 1971.

18. Collingwood TR: The effects of physical training upon behavior and self attitudes. *J Clin Psychol* 28: 583-585, 1972.

19. Hilyer JC, Mitchell W: Effect of systematic physical fitness training combined with counseling on the self concept of college students. *J Counseling Psychol* 26: 427-436, 1979.

BOOK REVIEWS

SPORTS MEDICINE—FITNESS, TRAINING, INJURIES, ed 2. Edited by Appenzeller O, Atkinson R. *Baltimore, Urban & Schwarzenberg, 1983, 441 pp., illus., $24.50.*

This new edition of the original 1981 presents a unique and more comprehensive approach to the area of sports medicine. A concise but interesting history of sport and medicine introduces the text. The format of the book consists of five sections, each composed of lectures given to physicians and medical students at the University of New Mexico School of Medicine. Section One discusses sports and the nervous system. A new chapter on the psychological and behavioral aspects of sports has been added to this section. Section Two, addressing the nutritional and gastrointestinal aspects of sport, now includes a lecture on fuel metabolism in the long distance runner. Hormone, fluid and electrolyte control is presented in Section Three. The lecture on exercise and the menstrual cycle has been expanded and more thoroughly documented. Section Four, as previously presented in edition one, discusses cardiovascular, pulmonary and hematologic effects of exercise. The Fifth section on locomotion has been broadened considerably to include new lectures on muscle testing, massage, stretching, biomechanics and injury treatment, and physical therapy for athletes.

Although twenty-six authors have contributed to the text, the material is well-organized and well-written. All information is presented in a logical and concise fashion with excellent current research support for all material. Each chapter has an extensive reference list. Most chapters are complemented by the utilization of graphs, tables or illustrations.

As in the first edition, the holistic approach to sports medicine is the most outstanding aspect of this book. Few available texts on sports medicine present the effect of sports on all bodily systems. This book defines sports medicine as knowledge and care of the total athlete. Thus, it fills a knowledge gap in the available literature on this specialized aspect of medicine.

The cost of this edition is also a definite plus. More information for a reduction in total price carries a very positive appeal.

The area of this text that could merit some improvement is the new chapter in the section on locomotion. Although the addition of the subject matter in these chapters is very relevant and indicated, the material presented is quite general and broad. More specific and research-documented information in all areas would most definitely improve the quality and validity of the new material. Any professional involved with sports medicine could understand and benefit from the content. While some chapters might be familiar and redundant to different readers, the other lectures present interesting, perhaps less known but equally pertinent subject matter for anyone involved in treatment of the total athlete.

Donna B. Bernhardt, MS, RPT, ATC
Assistant Professor
Boston University
Sargent College of Allied Health Professions

ADAPTED PHYSICAL EDUCATION: A PRACTITIONER'S GUIDE. By Masters LF, Mori AA, Lange EK. *Rockville, Aspen Systems Corporation, 1983, cloth, 387 pp., illus., $29.50.*

This book is designed to promote clearer definition of the physical education needs of the handicapped and to present practical methods for provision of these services. Chapters One through Six develop assessment and organizational theories while Chapters Seven through Ten present practical application methods.

The first chapter reviews the legal state of the art in adapted physical education and several potential service delivery systems. Chapter Two presents the salient aspects of a broad spectrum of cognitive and physical conditions. The third chapter identifies both informal and formal screening and diagnostic tools, and discusses interdisciplinary processing in formation of an individual educational program. An eight-step model for facilitating either the direct modeling/demonstration or the discovery/exploration approaches of instruction is presented in the fourth chapter.

Chapter Five thoroughly discusses all the organizational components of program and curriculum planning. The sixth chapter develops an overview of the basic developmental qualities of physical performance. Chapter Seven provides guidelines and fundamental instructional suggestions for games of low organization and for the Special Olympics, while Chapter Eight addresses prerequisites, instructional suggestions and adaptations for sports. Therapeutic recreation, rhythmic activities and dance are presented in Chapter Nine. The content of the last chapter includes aquatic instruction, emergency procedures and relaxation techniques. The appendices include a glossary, a short list of curriculum materials, sources of educational equipment, and resource centers and organizations for the disabled.

This guide is well-written and easily understandable. Material is concise, accurate, and presented in depth appropriate for the needs of the intended audience. The book is well-organized and very readable. An appropriate list of references follows every chapter. The chapters dealing with instructional skills contain a moderate number of instructional procedures. A multitude of tables outline activity components, purpose and necessary adaptations. A thorough list of various physical and mental conditions with suggested instructional adaptations is provided.

This book is recommended as a resource for physical education and special education teachers who work with the disabled. Developmental therapists could use the guide as a source of adapted games for all developmental levels. The manual would be an excellent introductory text for courses in adapted physical education.

Donna B. Bernhardt, MS, RPT, ATC
Assistant Professor
Boston University
Sargent College of Allied Health Professions

RECREATION EXPERIENCES FOR THE SEVERELY IMPAIRED OR NON-AMBULATORY CHILD. By Levine SP, Sharow N, Gaudette C, Spector S. *Springfield, IL, Charles C Thomas, Publisher, 1983, paper (spiral), 90 pp., illus., $11.75.*

This handbook provides the parents of severely impaired children with ideas for recreational experiences. Each activity has a list of materials needed, a description of the activity and what the experience provides for the child.

A section on movement activities describes various modes of pushing, pulling, rocking, rolling, swinging and carrying the child. The art and crafts activities include finger, mirror, sand, brush, blow, spray and splatter painting. Coloring, paper tearing, pasting, glittering and hand printing on plaster of paris is also described in this section. The music and listening chapter provides suggestions for tape recording, puppet making and dancing, and a description of body parts keeping time to music. The tactile sensory section offers ideas on the use of water, textured materials, fruits, soap bubbles, nerf balls, ice cubes, hair dryer, shaving cream and sand activities.

One chapter focuses on the social-psychological needs of the parent and family for recreation as well as their relationships with peers and the public. The last chapter gives some guidelines for developing a community-based recreation program for multiply impaired children. The appendix has some finger games that could be useful with severely impaired children.

The handbook's purpose of giving the parent of a severely impaired child some ideas for recreational experiences has been well accomplished. Its usefulness for the pediatric therapist, however, would be limited except as a reference to show to parents.

Elizabeth Stevenson, EdD, RPT, ATC, CCT
Division of Health and Physical Education
Physical Education Department
California State University, Sacramento

SPORTS FOR THE HANDICAPPED. By Allen A. *New York, Walker and Company, 1981.*

This brief text is divided into six chapters, each addressing a specific handicapped sport. The six sports included are skiing, wheelchair basketball, swimming, track and field, football and horseback riding. Each chapter presents an outstanding athlete and describes the adaptations necessary for their participation in a particular sport. The individuals highlighted include an amputee, a paraplegic, several blind persons, a deaf athlete and a child with cerebral palsy. Comments about the history of handicapped sports are concisely interwoven into the chapters.

This book features an easy reading style and a motivational theme. The information would be educational primarily for patients and their families. A listing of national and regional resources is provided for those interested in more detailed information.

David J. Miller, MS, LPT
Visiting Instructor
Division of Physical Therapy
University of North Carolina at Chapel Hill

SYMPOSIUM ON PEDIATRIC AND ADOLESCENT SPORTS MEDICINE. Edited by Betts JM, Eichelberger M. *Clinics in Sports Medicine 1(3). Philadelphia, WB Saunders, 1982.*

This publication presents a symposium of topics (excluding orthopedic injuries) which are relevant to the care of the young athlete. The stated objective of this collection of writings is to assist the pediatrician and the general practitioner in the diagnosis, treatment, and prevention of conditions which affect the adolescent athlete. Contributing authors take the positive approach that the dissemination of this knowledge is not intended to exclude youngsters from participation, but to insure safe participation for each athlete.

While the intended audience of this publication is pediatricians and general practitioners, other health care professionals (e.g., physical therapists, athletic trainers, nurses) interested in the care of the young athlete would benefit from the information presented. The section on epidemiology of sports injuries provides a powerful argument for continued epidemiologic studies aimed at identifying causal factors in athletic injuries, enabling preventive measures to be instituted. An article on preparticipation examinations of the young athlete gives excellent guidelines for group and individual examinations. Papers also present techniques for the nutritional and cardiologic assessment of the athlete. A section on the athlete with asthma and allergies reviews the physiology of these disorders and suggests guidelines for treatment which will maximize the participation of these youngsters.

Many of the articles in this symposium deal with on-the-field care of specific injuries. More technical information is then presented to assist the generalist or specialist who will provide care following initial first aid measures. Topics which are discussed include: dermatologic conditions, otolaryngologic injuries, dental and maxillofacial injuries, opthalmologic injuries, genitourinary injuries, drowning, and head and neck injuries. Emphasis is placed on rapid assessment of injury, delivery of appropriate care, and instituting measures which will prevent reoccurence of the injury. The symposium ends with a presentation of the possible relationship between mental health and exercise.

The collection of writings in this symposium is generally well-written and organized. The symposium contains excellent figures and tables which will facilitate the recognition and treatment of many of the injuries and conditions which are discussed. While a minimum of the materials are directed at physicians with specialized interests, the symposium should be of benefit to any generalist or health care professional interested in the care of the young athlete. Those who will benefit most from dissemination of this knowledge are young athletes, through safe participation in athletics.

Michael T. Gross, MS, LPT
University of North Carolina at Chapel Hill

DON'T FEEL SORRY FOR PAUL. By Wolfe B. *Philadelphia, JB Lippincott Company, 1974.*

The title of this book by Bernard Wolfe aptly describes the theme. The book verbally and visually depicts two weeks in the life of an eight year old boy, Paul, who was born with congenital deformities of both upper and lower limbs. Wolfe chronicles Paul's life both at school and at home. He realistically portrays Paul's encounters with his classmates, showing both the ridicule and the acceptance. By showing Paul playing football, roughhousing, horseback riding and doing art work, the author clearly demonstrates that Paul enjoys a multitude of activities that are age-appropriate. Wolfe depicts Paul's family as providers of the root of "normalcy." He verifies their encouragement and patience in permitting Paul to develop daily opportunities in independence. Wolfe interjects educational information about prosthetic usage and care that is particularly important for parents.

The beauty of this book lies in the depiction of Paul's life as normal, not sheltered and protected. Wolfe's excellent photography not only complements the text, but informs the reader. The pictures provide a heartwarming but appropriate emotional overtone. The result is a delightful resource for families and teachers of handicapped children.

Ruth Walker, LPT
Physical Therapy Department
North Carolina Memorial Hospital
Chapel Hill, NC

Recreational Resources

This section is designed to provide therapists involved or interested in recreation for disabled populations with a myriad of resources. The section will be divided into EQUIPMENT, PROGRAMS, and PUBLICATIONS/AUDIOVISUALS portions to facilitate usage. These resources are informational and educational, and can be used by both professionals and the public. I hope that this list will serve as a springboard for the learning of therapists and disabled individuals.

Donna B. Bernhardt, MS, RPT, ATC
Guest Editor

EQUIPMENT

Sports and Recreational Wheelchairs

1. Everest & Jennings, Inc., 1803 Pontius Ave., Los Angeles, CA 90025
2. Hale's Wheels, 15 Marlboro St., Belmont, MA 02178
3. Invacare Corporation, 1200 Taylor St, PO Box 4028, Elyria, OH 44036
4. Motion Designs, 1085 Cole Street, Clovis, CA 93612
5. Pep Company (Sportop by Ortop), 544 10th St., Palisades Park, NJ 07650
6. Production Research Corporation, 10217 Southard Dr., Beltsville, MD 20705
7. Quadra Wheelchairs, Inc., 31125 Via Colinas, Westlake Village, CA 91362
8. Sportschairs, 3673 Procyon Ave., Las Vegas, NV 89103
9. Stainless Medical Products, 9389 Dowdy Dr., San Diego, CA 92126
10. Theradyne Corporation, 21730 Hanover Ave., Lakeville, MN 55044

Bicycles and Tricycles

1. General Engines, Co., 591 Mantua Blvd., Sewell, NJ 08080
2. Daniel Gould Cycles, 723 Jackson, Missoula, MT 59801

3. Hedstrom Co., Bedford, PA 15522
4. Janssen USA, 2885 S. Santa Fe Dr., Englewood, CO 80110
5. New England Handcycles, Inc., 228 Winchester St., Brookline, MA 02146
6. Palmer Industries, PO Box 707, Union Station, Endicott, NY 13760
7. Unicycle, Inc., PO Box 276 Station N, Montreal, Canada H2X3M4

Wheelchair Rollers

State Aluminum, PO Box 987, Paramount, CA 90723

Gloves

Hawk Enterprises, Inc., PO Box 20490, San Jose, CA 95160

Sit Skis

1. Beneficial Design, Inc., 5858 Empire Grade, Santa Cruz, CA 95060
2. Mountain Man (Robert Pavlic), 720 Front St. Bozeman, MT 59715

Outriggers

1. Mountainsmith, Inc., 12790 W. 6th Place, Golden, CO 80401
2. New England Handicapped Sportsmen's Association, PO Box 2150, Boston, MA 02106

Chair Sled

Cardon, Inc., Dept 72, Arlington, WI 53911

Water Sports Devices

1. AMS, Inc. (swim lift), PO Box 548, Troy, MT 59935
2. Danmar Products (head support), 2390 Winewood, Ann Arbor, MI 48103
3. NEHSA (Kayaks, water skis), PO Box 2150, Boston, MA 02106

Hand Controls

1. Drive-Master Corp., 16A Andrews Dr., West Paterson, NJ 07424
2. Handicaps, Inc., 4335 So. Santa Fe Drive, Englewood, CO 80110
3. Kroepke Controls, Inc., 104 Hawkins St., Bronx, NY 10464
4. Nelson Medical Products, 5690-A Sarah Ave., Sarasota, FL 33581
5. Wells-Engberg Co., Inc., PO Box 6388, Rockford, IL 61125

Sports Leg Bag

Kay's Health Care Center, 4085 Tweedy Blvd., South Gate, CA 90280

Adapted Playing Cards

CIDCO Co., 6570 Devenwood Dr., Cincinnati, OH 45224

Handicapped Toys

Special Friends, PO Box 1262, Lowell, MA 01853

Shoe Exchange

Odd Shoe Size Exchange, PO Box 11212, San Francisco, CA 94101

Prosthetic Sports Feet

Seattle Prosthetics Research Study Center, Seattle, WA

Custom-designed Equipment

National Institute for Rehabilitation Engineering, 97 Decker Rd., Butler, NJ 07405

Table Tennis Gear

Recreation Unlimited, 820 Woodend Rd., Stratford, CT 06497

PROGRAMS

General Organizations with Sports Programs

1. AHPERD, Unit on Programs for the Handicapped, 1900 Association Dr., Reston, VA 22091
2. National Association of Sports for Cerebral Palsy, P.O. Box 3874 Amity Station, New Haven, CT 06511
3. National Spinal Cord Injury Foundation, 369 Elliot St., Newton Upper Falls, MA 02164
4. National Therapeutic Recreation Society, 1601 North Kent St., Arlington, VA 22209
5. National Wheelchair Athletic Association (NWAA), B. Dale Wiley, Chairman, 660 Capitol Hill Bldg., Nashville, TN 37179

6. Paralyzed Veterans of America, National Sports Coordinator, 4350 East-West Highway, Ste 900 Washington, D.C. 20014
7. President's Committee on Employment of the Handicapped, Subcommittee on Recreation & Leisure, 1111 20th St., N.W., Washington, D.C. 20036
8. University of Illinois, Rehabilitation-Education Center, 1207 So. Oak, Champaign, IL 61820
9. Vinland National Center, a healthsports center, 3675 Ihduhapi Rd., Loretto, MN 55357

Specific Sports Directory

All Terrain Vehicles

Wheelchair Motorcycle Association, Inc., 101 Torrey St., Brockton, MA 02401

Archery

1. National Wheelchair Athletic Association (NWAA), B. Dale Wiley, Chairman, 660 Capitol Hill Bldg., Nashville, TN 37179
2. National Archery Association, 1750 E. Boulder St., Colorado Springs, CO 80909

Basketball

National Wheelchair Basketball Association (NWBA), 110 Seaton Bldg., University of Kentucky, Lexington, KY 40506

Boating

Handicapped Boaters Association, PO Box 1134, Ansonia Station, NY 10023

Bowling

American Wheelchair Bowling Association (AWBA), 6718 Pinehurst Dr., Evansville, IL 47711

Flying

1. American Wheelchair Pilots Association, Attn: Dave Graham, P.O. Box 1181, Mesa, AZ 85201
2. Soaring Society of America, Inc., Box 66071, Los Angeles, CA 90066

Football

University of Illinois, Rehabilitation-Education Center, 1207 So. Oak, Champaign, IL 61820

Horseback Riding

North American Riding for the Handicapped Association, Box 100, Ashburn, VA 22011

Hunting and Fishing

Disabled Sportsmen of America, P.O. Box 26, Vinton, VA 24179

Marathon Racing

International Wheelchair Road Racers Club, Jeannette Parke, Central Office Manager, 12710 No. 30th St., #147, Tampa, FL 33612

Outdoor Recreation

1. Minnesota Outward Bound School, Box 250, Long Lake, MN 55356
2. Parcourse, Ltd., P.O. Box 99589, San Francisco, CA 94109
3. Sequoia Challenge, c/o Sally Murray, 2300 Bridgeway, Sausalito, CA 94965 (wilderness experience)
4. Winter Park Handicap Program, P.O. Box 313, Winter Park, CO 80482

River Rafting

American River Touring Association, 1016 Jackson St., Oakland, CA 94607

Scuba Diving

Truth Aquatics, Inc., Sea Landing Breakwater, Santa Barbara, CA 91309

Skiing

1. Colorado Outdoor Education Center, P.O. Box 697, Breckenridge, CO 80424
2. Winter Park Handicap Program, P.O. Box 313, Winter Park, CO 80482

Softball

National Wheelchair Softball Association, P.O. Box 737, Sioux Falls, SD 57101

Tennis

National Foundation of Wheelchair Tennis, Brad Parks, Chairman, 3857 Birch Street, Box 411, Newport Beach, CA 92660

Trapshooting

Mountain States Chapter Trap League (MSCTL), Attn: Lonnie Adkisson, c/o Mountain States Chapter, Paralyzed Veterans of America, Denver Federal Center, Denver, CO 80225

Volleyball

Wheelchair Volleyball, c/o Dennis Cherenko, 1200 Hornsby St., Vancouver, BC, Canada

Waterskiing

1. Disabled Services (Mike Bourgault), San Diego Recreation and Parks Dept., San Diego, CA
2. Easy Righter, 3N Company, Box 24500, Los Angeles, CA 90024

Weightlifting

Iron Athlete Training Center, Attn: Mark Lescoe, 1940 E. University Ave., Tempe, AZ 85281

Arts

1. Firebird Art Gallery, c/o Dennis Roach, 814 N. St. Asapho St., Alexandria, VA 22314
2. Performing Arts Theatre of the Handicapped (PATH), 5410 Wilshire Blvd., Suite 904, Los Angeles, CA 90036

Travel

1. Mobility International USA (MIUSA), PO Box 3551, Eugene, OR 97403
2. Whole Person Tours, 137 West 32nd St., Bayonne, NJ 07002

Accessibility

1. Accessibility Information Center, National Center for a Barrier Free Environment, Suite 1006, 1140 Connecticut Ave. NW, Washington, DC (800-424-2809)
2. Center for Education for Nontraditional Students, Inc (CENTS), c/o Patti Hague, 3130 Grimes Ave. N, Robbinsdale, MN 55422 (access awareness workshops for campuses)
3. Department of the Interior, 504 Coordinator, Bureau of Outdoor Recreation, Washington, DC 20240 (accessibility of outdoor recreation)
4. Higher Education and the Handicapped (HEATH), Project of the American Council on Education, One Dupont Circle, Suite 780, Washington, DC 20036 (college helpline for equal opportunities for disabled students)

AUDIOVISUALS—PUBLICATIONS

Audiovisuals

— "Two, Three Fasten Your Ski" (skiing for amputees)

— "The Mountain Does It for Me" (skiing for cerebral palsy)
Orthopedics Department
Handicapped Sports Program
Children's Hospital
1056 E. 19th Avenue
Denver, CO 80218

— "Celebrate" (sports for amputees, blind)
NEHSA
PO Box 2150
Boston, MA 02106

— "It's a New Day" (independent living and working)
Brookfield Productions
11600 Washington Place, Suite 203
Los Angeles, CA 90066

Publications

1. *Accent on Living Magazine,* Gillium Rd. and High Dr., PO Box 700, Bloomington, IL 61701.
2. Adams R, Daniel A, Rullman L: *Games, Sports and Exercises for*

the Physically Handicapped, ed 2. Philadelphia, Lea & Febiger, 1975.

3. Amary I: *Creative Recreation for the Mentally Retarded.* Springfield, IL, Charles C. Thomas, 1975.

4. *Aqua Dynamics: Physical Conditioning Through Water Exercises.* Washington, DC, US Government Printing Office, Superintendent of Documents, 1977.

5. Brightman A (ed): *Ordinary Moments: The Disabled Experience.* Baltimore, University Park Press, 1983.

6. Buell C: *Physical Education and Recreation for the Visually Handicapped.* Washington, DC, American Alliance for Health, Physical Education and Recreation, 1973.

7. Cohen S: *Special People.* Englewood Cliffs, NJ, Prentice-Hall, 1979.

8. Cordellos H: *Aquatic Recreation for the Blind.* Washington, DC, Physical Education and Recreation for the Handicapped Information and Research Utilization Center, 1976.

9. Cratty B, Breen J: *Educational Games for Physically Handicapped Children.* Denver, Love Publishers, 1972.

10. *Directory for Exceptional Children.* Boston, Porter Sargent, 1978.

11. *Directory of Organizations Interested in the Handicapped.* Washington, DC, People to People Program, 1976.

12. *Do It in Bed Exercise Program.* San Francisco, Healthright Publishing, 1982.

13. *Dressing Adaptations.* Stockton, CA, CHIC Press, 1980.

14. *Focus on Research: Recreation for Disabled Individuals.* Washington, DC, Regional Rehabilitation Research Institute on Attitudinal, Legal and Leisure Barriers, 1980.

15. Geddes D: *Physical Activities for Individuals with Handicapping Conditions,* edition 2. St. Louis, Mosby, 1978.

16. Grave N: *Challenging Opportunities for Special Populations in Aquatic, Outdoor and Winter Activities.* Washington, DC, Physical Education and Recreation for the Handicapped Information and Research Utilization Center, 1976.

17. *Green Pages Rehabilitation Sourcebook.* Winter Park, FL

18. Guttman L: *Textbook of Sport for the Disabled.* Aylesbury, England, HM and M, 1976.

19. Haskins J: *A New Kind of Joy: The Story of the Special Olympics.* Garden City, NY: Doubleday, 1976.

20. Hill K: *Dance for Physically Disabled Persons: A Manual for Teaching Ballroom, Square and Folk Dances to Users of Wheelchairs and Crutches.* Washington, DC, Physical Education and Recreation for the Handicapped Information and Research Utilization Center, 1976.

21. Hirst C, Michaelis E: *Developmental Activities for Children in Special Education.* Springfield, IL, Charles C. Thomas, 1972.
22. Hoffman R: *How to Build Special Equipment and Furniture for Handicapped Children.* Springfield, IL, Charles C. Thomas, 1970.
23. Kraus R: *Therapeutic Recreation Service: Principles and Practice.* Philadelphia, WB Saunders, 1983.
24. *Let's Play Games.* Chicago, National Easter Seal Society for Crippled Children and Adults, 1978.
25. Levine S: *Recreation Experiences for the Severely Impaired or Non-ambulatory Child.* Springfield, IL, Charles C. Thomas, 1983.
26. Marinelli R and Dell Orto A: *The Psychological and Social Impact of Physical Disability.* New York, Springer-Verlag, 1977.
27. Masters L, Mori A, Lange E: *Adapted Physical Education.* Rockville, MD, Aspen Systems Corp, 1983.
28. Miller A, Sullivan J: *Teaching Physical Activities to Impaired Youth: An Approach to Mainstreaming.* New York, Wiley, 1982.
29. *Parent's Guide to Accredited Camps.* Martinsville, IN, American Camping Association, 1981.
30. *Personal Computers for the Physically Handicapped.* Cupertino, CA, Apple Computer Inc., 1982.
31. *A Practical Guide for Teaching the Mentally Retarded to Swim.* Washington, DC, Council for National Cooperation in Aquatics, 1969.
32. *Publications for People with Disabilities, Professionals and Families.* Chicago, National Easter Seal Society for Crippled Children and Adults, 1983.
33. *Publications List.* Washington, DC, Regional Rehabilitation Research Institute on Attitudinal, Legal and Leisure Barriers, 1982.
34. Sosne M: *Handbook of Adapted Physical Education Equipment and its Use.* Springfield, IL, Charles C. Thomas, 1973.
35. *Special Olympics: Instructional Manual . . . from Beginners to Champions.* Washington, DC, American Association for Health, Physical Education and Recreation and Joseph Kennedy Foundation, 1972.
36. *Sports 'n Spokes Magazine,* 5201 North 19th Ave., Suite 111, Phoenix, AZ 85015.
37. Summerfield L: *Early Intervention for Handicapped Children Through Programs of Physical Education and Recreation.* Washington, DC, Physical Education and Recreation for the Handicapped Information and Research Utilization Center, 1976.
38. Thorum A: *Instructional Materials for the Handicapped: Birth through Childhood.* Salt Lake City, Olympus, 1976.
39. Tibaudo L: *Physical Activities for Impaired, Disabled, and Handicapped Participants.* Washington, DC, Physical Education and

Recreation for the Handicapped Information and Research Utilization Center, 1976.
40. Vannier M: *Physical Activities for the Handicapped.* Englewood Cliffs, NJ, Prentice-Hall, 1977.
41. Walter F: *Sports and Centres and Swimming Pools: A Study of their Design with Particular Reference to the Needs of the Physically Disabled.* Edinburgh, Thistle Foundation, 1971.
42. Wehman P (ed): *Recreation Programming for Developmentally Disabled Persons.* Baltimore, University Park Press, 1979.
43. Weisman M, Godfrey J: *Go Get On With It: A Celebration of Wheelchair Sports.* New York, Doubleday, 1976.
44. Zola I: *Missing Pieces.* Boston, Self Help Center, 1982.
45. Zola I (ed): *Ordinary Lives.* Boston, Self Help Center, 1982.